KT-150-770

MINISTRY IN THE LOCAL CHURCH

Edited by

Howard Belben

Centre for
Faith and Spirituality
Loughborough University

EPWORTH PRESS

David Belben

© Epworth Press 1986

All rights reserved. No part of this publication may
be reproduced, stored in a retrieval system, or
transmitted, in any form or by any means, electro-
nic, mechanical, photocopying, recording or otherwise, without the prior permission of the publisher,
Epworth Press.

British Library Cataloguing in Publication Data

Ministry in the local church.
  1. Pastoral theology——Methodist Church
(Great Britain)
I. Belben, Howard
253   BV4011

ISBN 0-7162-0415-0

First published 1986
by Epworth Press
Room 190, 1 Central Buildings,
Westminster, London SW1

Photoset by The Spartan Press Ltd
and printed in Great Britain by
Richard Clay (The Chaucer Press) Ltd,
Bungay, Suffolk

Contents

The Contributors

Peter W. Ensor	Lecturer in New Testament at St Paul's United Theological College, Lumuru, Kenya
John Horner	Superintendent minister of the Penzance Methodist Circuit
David H. Howarth	Minister in the Lytham Saint Annes Methodist Circuit
John Job	Superintendent minister of the Rugby and Daventry Methodist Circuit
Geoffrey Jones	Minister in the Radcliffe Methodist Circuit
I. Howard Marshall	Professor of New Testament Exegesis and Dean of the Faculty of Theology at the University of Aberdeen
Howard Mellor	Director of Evangelism at Cliff College, Calver, Sheffield
Stephen Mosedale	Minister in the Edinburgh and Forth Methodist Circuit
David G. Sharp	Minister in the Nantwich Methodist Circuit
A. Skevington Wood	Former Principal of Cliff College, Calver, Sheffield

Preface

The ten contributors to this book have all had experience as ministers of local Methodist churches. Though they write from different backgrounds and starting-points, they have in common a special interest in the evangelical approach to church life and ministry.

The writers aim to give, for readers of all denominations, a clear and coherent appraisal of the potential for ministry within each local church. They do not confine themselves to an account of the minister's role, but examine the ways in which church members today can minister to one another and to the world, and can face the challenge to expand and develop the work of the local church.

I am grateful for the help of the Reverend John Stacey of the Epworth Press, Doctor Stephen Travis and Doctor A. Skevington Wood, who have acted as editorial consultants, and all the contributors to this symposium.

HOWARD BELBEN
October 1985

THE LOCAL CHURCH

A. Skevington Wood

Our starting point, as we enquire about the status and significance of the local church in the setting of the twentieth century, must necessarily be the New Testament itself. This is at once the major source of information about Christian origins and, taken in conjunction with the preparatory revelation of God's purpose in the Old Testament, the determinative criterion not only of faith but of order as well. It is here that we discover what was the role of the local congregation in the primitive church, and what are the principles by which we may assess its effectiveness today.

Secular Use of Ekklēsia

Within the New Testament, we turn first to Acts 19 and its account of a riot which took place in Ephesus as a result of Christian preaching there. The church does not appear to be mentioned as such: instead we meet the Greek term *ekklēsia* (assembly) in its natural form, so to speak. It occurs three times – in verses 32, 39 and 41 – describing the crowd which gathered in the theatre after Demetrius the silversmith had roused his fellow-craftsmen and warned them that their livelihood was endangered by the missionaries. Luke may perhaps have had his tongue in his cheek when he called this confused rabble an *ekklēsia*. Certainly the town clerk did not regard it as an authentic assembly. In terms of local government, the *ekklēsia* was simply the electorate of a Greek city state officially summoned in its legislative capacity. It represented democracy in action within a specific territorial area.

The Ephesian mob was obviously an unauthorized assembly. It had convened itself, and the town clerk advised the principal objectors to resort to the assizes and the populace to raise the matter, should they still be dissatisfied, in the regular assembly (19.39).

If we are to arrive at what Emil Brunner regarded as 'the biblical self-understanding of *ekklēsia*', we must begin with this basic secular use of the term.[1] It means the statutory gathering of Greek citizens in any one place. The local limitation is implicit from the outset. In his play *The Acharnaians*, Aristophanes parodies a meeting of the *ekklēsia* in Athens, and from this and other sources it is possible to reconstruct what took place. Only those who had been deprived of civic rights (outlaws) or who never had any (slaves, women, children, aliens) were excluded. A herald (*keryx* – the New Testament word for a preacher) invited duly qualified electors to gather on the hill Pnyx near the Areopagus. Proceedings were opened with the offering of sacrifice by the priests and prayer to the gods. The *ekklēsia* was the governing body of Athens. Its decisions had to conform to the laws of the city state, but within these parameters its powers were virtually unlimited. Even recommendations of the Council (*boulē*) were submitted to the assembly for ratification.

This, then, was the provenance of the word adopted by the writers of the New Testament to denote the Christian church. We are not surprised to discover that here, too, its primary reference is to a local congregation. As Dean Alan Richardson observed, the factor of locality is a highly important feature in the New Testament doctrine of the church; it had been also in the Old Testament concept of the *qāhāl* (*ekklēsia* in the Septuagint) or congregation of Israel called out to meet in a particular place.[2] Indeed, the definitive unit of the Christian societary structure is the fellowship of believers meeting in one place.

Gospels and Acts

The term *ekklēsia* occurs twice in the gospels (Matt. 16.18; 18.17), but only once in relation to the church of Christ (the second reference being to the Jewish synagogue). It is of particular importance in the Acts of the Apostles and in the Pauline correspondence, including the pastorals. There are a few appearances elsewhere and as many as seventeen in the book of the Revelation. Although the actual word is not found in the letters of Peter, the idea is nevertheless present. We must therefore review the overall incidence of *ekklēsia* in the New Testament, enquiring how often it is employed to describe the local church.

In Acts *ekklēsia* recurs several times in the singular in connection with the mother church of Christianity in the holy city of Jerusalem (Acts 5.11; 8.1, 3; 11.22; 12.1, 5; 15.4, 22). This began as a single congregation, although no doubt others soon stemmed from it. Further occurrences are related to the local church in Syrian Antioch (Acts 13.1; 14.27; 15.3) and Ephesus (Acts 20.17, 28). The word also appears in the plural to describe a group of local churches in a particular region: those, for example, in Judaea, Galilee and Samaria (Acts 9.31, where the New English Bible translates with a collective singular), and again in Syria and Cilicia (Acts 15.41; 16.5, cf. v. 4).

Pauline Correspondence

The term *ekklēsia* is found in the letters of Paul more often than anywhere else in the New Testament, which is understandable since the apostle was the great missionary pioneer and church founder during this early period of development. Occasionally the singular is used in a general sense, as in Philippians 4.15 'no church entered into partnership with me' and I Corinthians 4.17 'as I teach them everywhere in every church'. The local church is clearly in view, but no specific location is identified.

In the great majority of instances, however, Paul names the place involved. He thus speaks about the *ekklēsia* in Thessalonica (I Thess. 1.1; II Thess. 1.1), in Corinth (I Cor. 1.2; II Cor. 1.1), in nearby Cenchreae (Rom. 16.1) and in Laodicea (Col. 4.16). Moreover, when he urges the Corinthians to 'give no offence to Jews or to Greeks or to the church of God', (I Cor. 10.32), he is thinking in the first place about the local situation in which abuses in worship were causing a scandal both within the assembly and beyond it. Similarly in I Corinthians 11.22,

Paul warns against bringing the church of God into contempt because of such excesses. In I Corinthians 11.18 the divisions Paul deplores are apparent when the believers 'assemble as a church'. The discussion of spiritual gifts in chapters twelve and fourteen is set in the context of what happens when the local congregation meets (I Cor. 12.28; 14.5, 12, 19, 23, 28, 35). 'The underlying and primitive meaning', explains Pierre Benoit, 'is that of the assembly of the faithful thought of in a concrete way'.[3] Even the reference in Romans 16.23 to 'the whole church' has a local application to the Christians in Corinth (from which Paul wrote to the capital) where Gaius exercised his Christian hospitality.

In a few cases *ekklēsia* is employed by Paul in the singular to describe a house fellowship. There was one in the home of Prisca and Aquila in Rome (Rom. 16.5; I Cor. 16.19); another where Archippus lived in Colosse (Philemon 2); and a third in Laodicea at the residence of Nymphas (or Nympha) as mentioned in Colossians 4.15. There are other instances, of course, where *ekklēsia* denotes the universal or even, on occasion, the ideal church. It is especially in the letters to the Ephesians and Colossians that Paul speaks like this.

Paul is equally liberal in his use of the plural form 'churches'. Many of the occurrences are general – 'all the churches' (I Cor. 7.17), 'all the churches of Christ' (Rom. 16.16), 'all the churches of the saints' (I Cor. 14.33, cf. v. 34), 'the churches of God' (I Cor. 11.16; II Thess. 1.4). Some are applied, as in Acts, to the local congregations within a specific geographical area – 'the churches of Christ in Judaea' (Gal. 1.22; cf. I Thess. 2.14), 'the churches of Asia' (I Cor. 16.19 – the Roman province of Asia is meant, not the entire continent), 'the churches of Galatia' (I Cor. 16.1; Gal. 1.2), 'the churches of Macedonia' (II Cor. 8.1).

Lucien Cerfaux advances the theory that the phrase 'the churches of God' originally represented a technical formula to denote the Christian communities in Jerusalem and Judaea (cf. I Thess. 2.14).[4] This might perhaps account for the distinction in I Corinthians 11.16 between Paul's own practice in the Gentile congregations and those observed in the Palestinian churches. In Romans 16.4 the apostle explicitly associates himself with 'all the churches of the Gentiles' as an ethnic group. Cerfaux furthermore claims that the singular title 'church of God' was first applied to the Jerusalem community itself as being a prototype.[5] Each local congregation in Judaea, and eventually beyond it, was regarded as a living cell reproducing the features of its parent. Thus, when Paul confessed to the Galatians that he 'persecuted the church of God', he meant that before his conversion he harried the Christians in Jerusalem.

Pastorals and Revelation

The three occurrences in the pastorals, which some scholars believe to have been written by an unknown author, fall into line with the usage already described in the undisputedly Pauline epistles. In I Timothy 3.5 the church of God, for which the bishop has responsibility as the chief elder, does not as yet cover a regional diocese but is simply a local congregation of Christians regarded, according to the parallelism of the passage, as a single household. Equally in I Timothy 5.16, the church that is to be relieved of responsibility for widows, since there are relatives to care for them, is typical yet specific. Even 'the church of the living God' in I Timothy 3.15, which is referred to as 'the pillar and bulwark of the truth', is the household of believers in a given place. What supports and protects the gospel is the faithful witness of the local church.

Apart from Acts and the Pauline correspondence, the *ekklēsia* appears most frequently in the book of the Revelation. All but one of the seventeen references occur in the first three chapters, which are related to the seven churches in Asia – Ephesus, Smyrna, Pergamum, Thyatira, Sardis, Philadelphia and Laodicea. In Revelation 22.16 'all the churches' (i.e. of Asia) receive the testimony of Jesus through his messenger. A comprehensive statistical analysis reveals that in fifty-nine cases in the New Testament *ekklēsia* refers to a local assembly in one place. In thirty-six cases it refers to these communities in the plural. In fifteen cases it apparently refers to the universal church (either actual or ideal), although, as Cerfaux claims, never without the local church also in mind.

Local and Universal

This leads us to consider how the New Testament understands the relationship between the local and the universal church. Recent investigations have clarified the issue to a marked degree, with important practical consequences as we seek to rediscover the role of the congregational unit today. No single body of believers is itself *the* church (i.e. the total church) but each nevertheless represents and reflects it as the church in that place. The local church is seen as a microcosm of the universal church; or, to put it the other way round, the universal church finds its local manifestation in each individual *ekklēsia*. According to the Arndt-Gingrich Lexicon, 'the local as well as the universal church is more specifically called *ekklēsia tou theou* (the church of God) or *ekklēsia tou christou* (the church of Christ). This is essentially Pauline usage, and it serves to give the current Greek term its Christian colouring and thereby its specific meaning'.[6]

As Hans Küng brings out in a most perceptive treatment of the biblical evidence summarized above, this concept carries with it two significant implications.[7] In the first place, the local church is not to be regarded as a section or a province of the whole church. It is in no sense merely a sub-division of the real church which, as a wider body, must therefore be treated as superior. Küng adds:

> It is an unfortunate fact that the word 'church' is habitually used to describe the whole *ekklēsia* – this is one consequence of an abstract and idealizing concept of the Church as though the Church were not *wholly* present in every place, endowed with the *entire* promise of the gospel, and an *entire* faith, recipient of the *undivided* grace of the Father, having present in it an *undivided* Christ and enriched by the *undivided* Holy Spirit. No, the local church does not merely belong to the Church, the local church is the Church (italics Küng's).[8]

Küng insists that the whole church can only be understood in terms of the local church and its concrete actions. The local church is not a tiny cell of a larger organism, which does not really represent it and has no purpose in itself. It is in fact the real church to which, in its own localized situation, everything is given and promised which it needs for the salvation of men and women: the preaching of the gospel, the sacraments, varying gifts and ministries.

The second implication is that the whole *ekklēsia* is not a collection or association of accumulated local churches. These are related to each other by something more than external structures and administration. They are internally linked in the unity of the faith. 'The Church is not a limited company, or organization of individual communities; the *ekklēsia* is not made by adding together the local churches, nor can it be broken down into them. Rather, the *ekklēsia* of God exists in each place'.[9]

The precise designation of the local church in the New Testament is instructive. There is not, for example, a Corinthian church, or a church of the Corinthians, or a church of Corinth, but 'the church of God which is at Corinth' (I Cor. 1.2; II Cor. 1.1). 'Each *ekklēsia*, each congregation, community, church, however small, however poor, however insignificant', adds Küng, 'is a full and perfect manifestation of *the ekklēsia*, the congregation, the community, *the* Church of God'.[10]

Body of Christ

All this ties in with what the New Testament understands by the body of Christ. A body is essentially a localized presence. Paul's analogy is applied to the church in Corinth (I Cor. 12.12–27). The members are individual Christians fulfilling their diversified functions. Each local church is the body of Christ in that place. It is a fellowship of the Spirit in which every member is allotted his special gift and corresponding ministry. 'There is not in addition a further "organization"', explained Emil Brunner, 'for the Body of Christ organizes itself. It is just for this reason that it is called the *Body* of Christ. Above all there are no legal regulations which – as in the essence of law – might be considered to have a formal validity, so that because "it has been so laid down" things must henceforward take the course which "has been laid down". On the contrary that is by the nature of things excluded in the *ekklēsia* . . .

Although the brotherhood is composed of quite ordinary men, it is not ordered by the will and law of men, but simply and solely by the Spirit *(pneuma)*, His gifts and grace *(charismata)* and His ministries *(diakoniai)'.*[11] As Brunner realized, such a concept may be dismissed all too easily as utopian, but he saw it as the necessary outcome of Paul's understanding of the gospel 'and therefore as the necessary norm for all time of the believing fellowship of Christians, who are conscious that they have their foundation in Jesus Christ alone'.[12]

Clearly this emphasis on the freedom of the Spirit in the body of Christ needs to be counter-balanced by those passages in the New Testament which speak about the oversight of the church and the proper ordering both of worship and community life. But when adequate allowance has been made for this disciplinary factor, which we dare not ignore, we are nevertheless compelled to conclude that the local congregation is intended to be an active and creative fellowship in which the Holy Spirit ensures that the ministry of our Lord himself is still carried on through his body the church.

We are now in a position to spell out in practical terms what the local church was meant to be as we meet it in the pages of the New Testament. How these factors can be rediscovered and reinterpreted in the 1980s ought to be discussed in every church council.

1. A Focal Point for Worship

By definition the *ekklēsia* is a called-out company of God's people. They are not convened without a purpose but primarily in order to glorify the Lord. The stress lies on meeting with an end in view. 'A church is an assembly of Christians', explains Cerfaux, 'the bringing together in *act* of the local church'.[13] That act is the offering of worship in prayer and praise, in the preaching of the word and in the breaking of bread. This will be the highlight of the weekly programme. 'In order that she shall accomplish anything the church must live', declared E. R. Micklem, 'and her life depends on her worship'.[14] It is at the local level that this vitality is to be sustained. The health of the whole church is determined by the strength of congregational worship in each place where Christians gather to acknowledge the Lord.

2. A Training School for Discipleship

We hear a good deal in these days about what it means to be a disciple of Jesus and the importance of making disciples in the context of church growth. A disciple is one who learns. He goes to school with Christ as his teacher. The classroom is the local church. Here he takes on his shoulders the yoke of the gospel as the Jewish initiate accepted the yoke of the law (Matt. 11.29, 30). Our Lord's own master plan was to train twelve men to carry on his mission. Each local church should be a teaching centre in which new converts are prepared for active membership in the body of Christ and equipped for outreach to others. Discipleship involves discipline, and committed Christians, however young in the faith, will evidence the reality of their relationship to Christ as they seek to know the faith by studying the Bible and how to grow in grace as they are taught the art of prayer.

3. A Proper Sphere for Ministry

The gifts of the Spirit are to be exemplified and exercised within the body of Christ. In the New Testament such ministry is mostly localized. There were, of course, those who went from place to place like the missionary apostles and accredited evangelists. Their task was to preach Christ where he had never been named before (Rom. 15.20) and to plant churches. Once new churches had been founded, they moved on, and their ministry was then continued by the membership. Writing to the Christians in Corinth, Paul underlines the fact that 'within our community' (I Cor. 12.28, NEB; 'in the church', RSV.) God has appointed apostles, prophets, teachers, miracle-workers, healers, helpers, administrators and speakers in various kinds of tongues. The local church should be a dynamic fellowship of the Spirit in which the gifts and ministries of individual believers are encouraged and enabled to flourish and increase.

4. A Launching-pad for Mission

The evangelization of Judaea and Samaria was undertaken from the mother church in Jerusalem. The Gentile mission was inaugurated from Antioch in Syria. It was while the members of the congregation there, including certain prophets and teachers, were keeping a fast and offering worship to the Lord, that the Holy Spirit led them to set apart Paul and Barnabas for the work to which he had called them (Acts 13.1–3). When the first missionary itinerary was completed the apostles returned in order to report back to base at Antioch. The whole congregation was summoned to hear about 'all that God had done with them, and how he had opened a door of faith to the Gentiles' (Acts 14.27). The urge to evangelism should be inherent in the local church. When the body of Christ in any one place is alive and alert, no external stimulus is needed.

5. A Testing Ground for Love

It has been said that Calvary is the academy of love. There at the cross we learn its meaning. The church is the factory of love. There we produce it and check it for quality, before it is exported to the world in the form of compassionate concern for those in need. Here is the badge by which genuine Christians are identified. 'By this all men will know that you are my disciples', said Jesus, 'if you have love for one another' (John 13.35). From this mutual love flows mutual forbearance (Eph. 4.2), mutual forgiveness (Eph. 4.32), mutual encouragement (I Thess. 4.18; 5.11), mutual incitement to service (Heb. 10.24, 25), mutual confession and intercession (James 5.16) and mutual burdenbearing (Gal. 6.2).

> Hence may all our actions flow,
> Love the proof that Christ we know;
> Mutual love the token be,
> Lord, that we belong to thee. (Charles Wesley)[15]

The life of the local church should prompt unbelievers to exclaim, without a hint of derision: 'See how these Christians love!'

We have indicated how the New Testament envisages the relationship between the local and the universal church. It is clear that local churches enjoyed fellowship with each other within the same geographical area and indeed further afield. We think of the extensive Christian hospitality which was such a prominent feature of the apostolic age and the famine relief fund raised by Paul from the Gentile communities for the church in Jerusalem. What is more difficult to determine from scripture is how the local church should stand *vis à vis* its denomination, for, of course, such an association did not then obtain. Indeed, Victor de Waal takes the view that the distinctive sub-cultures within Christianity – Catholicism, Anglicanism, Presbyterianism, Methodism and the rest – all too often effectively hinder the local church from fulfilling its true function in the environment in which it is set.[16]

On the other hand, we must remember, as we have seen above, that in New Testament times local churches did not remain in detachment from one another. They were linked not only in ministry and pastoral concern but to a certain degree in discipline as well. The Jerusalem Council, described in Acts 15, showed that joint discussions were found to be necessary, leading to agreed guidelines for general practice. As Julian Charley concludes, the impression given is that the early church combined elements both of independency and of connexionalism.[17] Nowadays we need to rediscover how they can co-exist. In the first century the danger was that of undue fragmentation: in ours it is that of over-centralization.

Since the New Testament presents a picture of unity in diversity, something must be said very briefly in closing about the pluriformity of the church. Within the essential oneness of the Christian community there is room for rich variety. That is the case both within the local congregation and beyond in the extended family of the universal church. As there are different kinds of gifts, but the same Spirit, so there are different kinds of service, but the same Lord, and different kinds of work, but the same God who inspires them all in every one (I Cor. 12.4, 5).

Historically, this innate pluriformity has in fact tended to produce division and indeed separation. But it was not designed to do so, and there is no need for that to happen. In our fear of disruption we must not shrink from exploring the many forms in which communal faith can be expressed. Such diversity reflects the character of God himself, whose wisdom is vividly depicted in Ephesians 3.10 as being multicoloured.

Even though we may not wholly agree with the thesis propounded by Ernst Käsemann and others that the New Testament itself contains a series of disparate and even contradictory theologies, it has to be recognized nevertheless that the one gospel has been variously understood and interpreted at certain points and in different periods of history. Since our knowledge at best is imperfect (I Cor. 13.9), we can never claim a monopoly of the truth and must always be open to insights other than our own within the realm of revelation. There is, however, a vital distinction to be maintained at every level of the church's life, between a valid biblical pluriformity and an unlicensed pluralism which may too easily degenerate into a theological free-for-all.

Notes

1. Charles W. Kegley (ed.), *The Theology of Emil Brunner*, Library of Living Theology Vol III, Macmillan 1962, p. 347.
2. Alan Richardson, *An Introduction to the Theology of the New Testament*, SCM Press 1958, p. 288.
3. Pierre Benoit, 'L'horizon paulinien de l'epître aux Ephésiens', *Revue Biblique*, Vol. xlvi, 1937, p. 357.
4. Lucien Cerfaux, *The Church in the Theology of St Paul*, ET, Nelson 1959, pp. 115–116.
5. Cerfaux, op. cit., pp. 114–117.
6. William F. Arndt and F. Wilbur Gingrich (eds), *A Greek-English Lexicon of the New Testament*, University of Chicago Press 1957, p. 240.
7. Hans Küng, *The Church*, ET, Search Press 1968, p. 85.
8. Ibid.
9. Küng, op. cit., p. 86.
10. Ibid.
11. Emil Brunner, *The Christian Doctrine of the Church, Faith and the Consummation*, Dogmatics Vol. III, ET, Lutterworth Press 1962, p. 45.
12. Brunner, op. cit., p. 46.
13. Cerfaux, op. cit., p. 189.
14. Edward R. Micklem, *Our Approach to God: A Study in Public Worship*, Hodder and Stoughton 1934, p. 11.
15. *Hymns and Psalms* 756, v. 11.
16. Victor de Waal, *What is the Church?*, SCM Press 1969, p. 58.
17. Julian Charley, 'Church Order', *Unity in Diversity*, ed. A. Morgan Derham, Evangelical Alliance 1966, p. 20.

2

THE MINISTRY

I. Howard Marshall

Introduction

If the local church today is ineffective in its work and witness, the causes may lie both in the individuals who compose it and also in the structure which determines and shapes their activity. Our concern in the present essay is primarily with the second of these factors. One approach to our problem would be to discuss what the church ought to be doing today and to frame a structure in the light of this. But, however much the details of church structure must be determined by the contemporary situation, the 'shape' of the church must be determined by the pattern which we discover in the New Testament, and, as members of an *ecclesia semper reformanda*, a church which must continually be reforming itself in the light of scripture, we must look to the New Testament for guidance and direction.

Our problem is to sort out what is of permanent validity in the New Testament understanding of the ministry, and what is merely the first-century manner of expression of the basic character of ministry, and to apply the former to our situation. In what follows, therefore, we shall distinguish the variable factors in the New Testament picture from the constant elements, and then make some comments on the contemporary situation. However, an important principle which we shall emphasize is that the very variety in the New Testament picture is an important factor – a constant – in the structure of the church, and that we need to recover this today.

Variable Factors in the New Testament Concept of Ministry

The word used for 'ministry' in the New Testament is *diakonia*, which basically means 'service'. Along with the associated words for 'minister' and 'to minister' it is used in three ways: (1) It refers to the work of Jesus himself (Mark 10.45; Luke 22.27). (2) It refers to service of all kinds in the church, carried on by a variety of people (e.g. I Cor. 12.5; Eph. 4.11ff.; Heb. 6.10; Rev. 2.19). (3) The word developed a narrower meaning as a technical term for one particular kind of service, that of the 'deacon' (Rom. 16.1; Phil. 1.1; I Tim. 3.8, 12). 'Ministry' is thus a very general concept. It signifies any kind of service performed in the church by people who are serving their heavenly Lord and also serving their fellow-Christians as the objects of their care. As a result, the exercise of ministry shows considerable variety.

1. One Minister or Many Ministers?

In New Testament times the task of ministry was carried on by a large number of people. The use of the term 'minister' was not confined to certain people who held one particular kind of office in the church. The term *diakonos* is used in a broad sense for service in the church, and also in a narrow sense; but when the latter sense developed, it was not used for the people whom we now call ministers. In fact we render *diakonos* in this technical sense by 'deacon'. Our modern restriction of the term 'minister' to a particular group of workers in the church who do not correspond to the New Testament deacons is unjustifiable, and it has the effect of suggesting that only '*the* minister' acts as '*a* minister' within the church. It would seem that our modern usage of 'minister' does not reflect the New Testament *diakonos* but the later *klērikos*.

2. Full-time or Part-time Ministers?

The New Testament does not show the modern distinction between full-time and part-time workers in the church, or between paid and unpaid workers. Naturally there were people who were fully engaged in the work of the church and some of them travelled extensively in missionary work. Such men had both the need and the right to be supported by the churches because they were not able to work for their living (I Cor. 9.3–14; Gal. 6.6; III John 5–8). But we find that Paul worked part-time at a craft so as not to be a burden on the churches (I Cor. 9.12, 15; I Thess. 2.6). In the case of local church workers there is insufficient evidence to show which, if any of them, were engaged full-time in this work, although in some cases church leadership entitled a man to payment (I Tim. 5.17f. is generally interpreted in this way).

We are not told whether the call to ministry was to a life-long office. This may well have been normally the case, and there is no reason to suppose that an apostle could cease to be an apostle (even if he retired from active service). Since, however, the New Testament is silent on the matter generally, it is an area in which there are no binding rules.

3. Itinerant or Local?

The distinction between itinerant and local ministries was a fluid one. Philip seems to have changed from being an itinerant to a settled minister, and it is hard to tell whether prophets were a local or an itinerant group; probably both kinds existed.

4. Uniformity or Variety?

The pattern of ministry varied considerably throughout the New Testament churches. Even within the writings of Paul we have evidence of variety: the 'bishops and deacons' at Philippi bear no correspondence to the lists of ministerial functions and charismatic gifts in I Corinthians 12. The pictures given by Acts and the Johannine epistles are different again. It is generally agreed that there is no such thing as *the* New Testament pattern of ministry.

5. Ordained or Non-ordained?

There was no distinction drawn between clergy and laity in the New Testament church. Clearly certain people, such as the apostles, did form a special group within the church by reason of their unique functions, and others were appointed to special ministries by the laying on of hands. But laying on of hands was not a uniform rite throughout the churches for every person who performed tasks of ministry, and a wide variety of functions were all reckoned equally as ministries for which the Spirit equipped people according to his will without any special human rites of recognition.

These five points indicate that at every point where it seems possible flexibility and variety characterized the New Testament picture of ministry, and it will be obvious that these characteristics are not present to anything like the same extent in the local church today. Of course it can be argued that variety was only natural in a group of young churches, and that by the second century and onwards the picture was becoming much more uniform; perhaps we ought to be guided more by the finished product than by the undeveloped first-century churches. While, however, variety simply for variety's sake may be a bad thing, the New Testament pattern may have something important to teach us. What we have is a church adapting itself to the needs of each local situation and to the resources which it possessed, and this picture suggests that the local church today needs to be equally adaptable.

Constants in the New Testament Concept of Ministry

Faced by this variety of expression, we now need to consider whether there are any constants in the picture, any factors which appear sufficiently frequently to enable us to claim that these are important, basic aspects of ministry which must be preserved, however varied may be the ways in which they come to expression.

1. Service and Humility

The purpose of ministry is humble service. This is evident from the meaning of the word itself, and it is emphasized by the example and teaching of Jesus (Mark 10.42–45; Luke 22.24–27; Mark 9.35; Matt. 23.10–12; John 13.14–16). Ultimately the service is rendered to God; ministry is done in obedience to the Lord. But it is a service done to people in that they are the recipients of the service. At the same time, the person who serves is to regard himself as the servant of those whom he serves (Mark 9.35; 10.43; Luke 22.26f.); he is not to think highly of himself or of his own interests, but is to serve the needs of others. Yet this does not mean that those served are to consider themselves the masters of those who serve them, or that the servant is to place the interests of people above those of the Lord (Gal. 1.10).

2. *The Tasks of Ministry*

When Jesus appointed his twelve disciples, they were 'to be with him, and to be sent out to preach and have authority to cast out demons' (Mark 3.14f.). The first thought here is probably of personal aid to Jesus in his work, but it is difficult to avoid the implication that the twelve were to learn by their association with him how to work for him on their own. The second aspect of their role was the same as that of Jesus who preached the gospel and healed the sick. We may see here a basic role in Jesus' lifetime of evangelistic proclamation of the message of the kingdom accompanied by the performance of the mighty works that demonstrated the reality of God's kingly rule. In Acts we see the same pattern present. The apostles are committed to a task of preaching and teaching, which has widened out from that in the gospels to include instruction of believers as well as evangelism. The message is accompanied by mighty works, and a new element is the care of the poor within the church, which eventually proves to be so time-consuming that it threatens to interfere with their prayer and teaching. It is therefore necessary to appoint others to help with the work, and, although the seven appointed were ostensibly intended to 'serve tables', at least two of them were in fact extremely active as evangelists. It would seem that the task of teaching and preaching is of primary importance, and that the care of the poor – who are apparently the poor within the church – is secondary to this. The same pattern is repeated in the case of Paul who is again a preacher and teacher, but whose epistles also reveal his active part in raising money for the poor in Jerusalem. The pattern in I Peter 4.11 also mentions speaking and service. We may take it that these two aspects of ministry were a recognized part of the work, but it is significant that in I Peter they can be allotted to different people, and the same point would seem to be suggested by Paul's listing of the variety of spiritual gifts in I Cor. 12.

Two other aspects of ministry are important. First, the example of the apostles (Acts 6.4) and of Paul (e.g. Rom. 1.9) indicates that prayer for those who are served is an important element in ministry. Second, those who acted as ministers also had responsibilities as leaders in the churches. They were to be treated with the respect due to their office, and obedience is even mentioned in this connection (Heb. 13.17). 'Leadership' is a vague word, and perhaps we ought to substitute some such phrase as 'pastoral care' in order to bring out the element which seems to be uppermost in New Testament thinking (II Cor. 11.28; Heb. 13.17; I Pet. 5.2f.).

One task which is conspicuous by its absence is the administration of the sacraments. We are simply not told who carried out baptisms or presided at the Lord's Supper. This silence could be accidental; it may have been so self-evident that the church 'leaders' carried out these functions that nothing needed to be said. Paul certainly thought that so far as he personally was concerned his task was preaching rather than baptizing (I Cor. 1.17).

3. The Appointment of Ministers

The ways by which people became ministers were very varied. On the one hand, there are cases where persons were evidently possessed of spiritual gifts and appear to have exercised them simply because they had them. At the same time, the instructions which Paul gave to the church at Corinth suggest that the church could exercise a measure of control over the use of these gifts, such as tongues and prophecy. On the other hand, we have examples of needs to be met, and persons being appointed to meet them. The appointment of local church leaders was of this nature. It does not make a lot of difference whether we think of the Spirit taking the initiative in moving the church to take action (Acts 13.1–3) or of the church seeing a need and seeking the Spirit's guidance in taking action (Acts 6.1–6). In both cases it is recognized that ministers are appointed ultimately by God.

In any case, it is apparent that in the choice of ministers the churches looked for people with spiritual qualities that were expressed in moral uprightness and with the necessary capacities for the particular task envisaged (I Tim. 3.1–13).

4. The Corporate Exercise of Ministry

In the New Testament ministry is a corporate activity involving several persons in the local church. There always seems to be a plurality of persons exercising ministry in a church, some of them local, some of them itinerant, each performing different tasks according to the gifts bestowed on them by the Spirit and/or in terms of a particular function assigned to them. Even in the comparatively formal situation reflected in the pastoral epistles there is a differentiation between bishops and deacons, although it is difficult to be sure precisely what the differences between them were.

The New Testament and the Local Church Today

Now that we have seen something of both the variety of expressions of ministry in the early church and the constant factors which were present, we have the task of asking how ministry should be carried on in the local church today. At the outset it can be said that there is a fairly obvious correspondence between practice in the Methodist Church and the kind of New Testament pattern that has been outlined. At some important points, however, the correspondence could be improved.

1. Developing a New Attitude to Ministry

A major weakness in the life of the local church today arises from the fact that we have limited the term 'minister' to one kind of person who performs service in the church and, in general, to only one particular person in any given church. This has been an unfortunate development. Basically, it has led to a frame of mind which thinks of ministry purely in terms of what 'the minister' does and thus loses the sense that other tasks in the church are equally tasks of ministry. Although the New Testament church apportioned the different tasks of ministry among different persons, we have reached the point where most of them are assigned to one person. This is undesirable. On the one hand, it expects one man to be able to demonstrate a variety of gifts, whereas in practice few people can be expected to show omnicompetence in the varied tasks of ministry. On the other hand, it stifles the gifts that have been distributed by the Spirit to other members of the congregation. We recognize in practice that there are different gifts of the Spirit assigned to lay preachers and to class or group leaders and pastoral visitors, although of course there are some individuals who can happily combine both duties. It seems doubtful whether we should expect that each 'minister' (in the traditional sense) should be competent in both areas.

What is needed is a new mentality in which it is recognized that ministry is the task of many members of the church, and it would be helpful if we could stop thinking and speaking of 'the minister' in a sense which suggests that the task of ministry is uniquely his. It might be best to drop the term altogether, and with it our curious habit of dressing 'the minister' differently from other Christians. I realize that this is a fairly revolutionary proposal, and that it has wider implications, especially in view of the practice of the church worldwide, but it may be worth noting that such groups as the Society of Friends and the Brethren are successful examples of an understanding of ministry that we should seriously consider.

2. The Need for Opportunities and Training

What we ought to be seeking for is a pattern of local church life in which many persons participate in ministry, and which actively encourages people to use the gifts with which the Spirit equips them. Most churches already have something along these lines in their structure of lay preachers, pastoral visitors, Sunday school teachers, youth workers, and so on. The point is that this pattern should grow and develop even more.

On the one hand, this will mean providing more opportunities for people to take part in ministry. There could, for example, be much more participation in the conduct of church services, so that these truly become corporate activities and the congregation really do share in both giving and receiving. The task of pastoral visitation could be shared out much more effectively among several people, with the result that the church would be much more of a caring community. Moreover, as the members of the church become more aware of their gifts and seek opportunities to use them, there will surely be an increase in outreach by the church.

On the other hand, it will be necessary to provide training in the use of spiritual gifts and the exercise of ministry. Probably the major difference between 'the minister' and the other members of the congregation is that he alone has had a training in theology, both theoretical and practical; only the local preachers have had anything comparable. The church would be immensely strengthened if its members could be trained for the various tasks of ministry, and it is arguable that the limited resources available for ministerial training at a denominational level should be redeployed to provide far more of what we at present call 'lay training'. As the number of candidates for 'the ministry' has declined in recent years, the church's response should not have been to cut back the amount of ministerial training but rather to increase the proportion of 'lay training'.

The development of so-called part-time and auxiliary ministries would fit in with this pattern. An increasing number of people may well be able to do a secular job part-time and serve in the church part-time. They would stand between those who serve the church full-time and those who do a secular job full-time and serve the church in their leisure-time. To attempt to formalize these three basic types of approach with the aid of such terms as 'auxiliary ministry' could, however, be unhelpful; they smack of second-class citizenship. Rather we should recognize a spectrum of ministerial tasks extending from full-time to leisure-time activity.

3. Preserving Variety at the Local Level

The New Testament pattern indicates that different local churches do not need to have the same ministerial structure, but must adapt to local needs and resources. There is, for example, a monolithic uniformity in Methodism which can be a danger at this point. To discuss the Methodist pattern of church organization would take us away from the specific topic of ministry, but the topics are not unrelated. Specifically, it is a pity that recent changes in structure and nomenclature have led to an organization of the church by a series of 'committees' with fairly elaborate methods of representation and appointment. The whole thing is reminiscent of local government or industrial management and conveys the sense of 'managing' the church. We need to be careful lest the character of the set-up subtly destroys the idea of 'ministry' which should motivate those who serve in it. It is here that the traditional Methodist term 'steward' has much to commend it as a means of reminding church leaders of the nature of their task as servants of God entrusted with the care of his church.

4. Getting our Priorities in Ministry Right

(a) Building up the congregation. The task of ministry is primarily a spiritual one. It is concerned with the 'building up' of the people of God. It is noteworthy that the information we have about Christian meetings in the New Testament implies that their primary function was the building up of the congregation rather than the worship of God. This is not to say that the latter element was lacking; rather the nurture of the congregation was the uppermost reason for gathering together. Our modern tendency to lay the emphasis on worship is in danger of placing the stress in the wrong place. A major emphasis in New Testament gatherings of Christians lies on teaching and instruction in the faith as a means of spiritual nurture. This emphasis needs to be recovered in an age which ascribes a subordinate (and brief) place to the sermon. The sermon in the traditional sense is not of course the only means of Christian teaching, but it, or some other mode of instruction which has the same aim, should be central in the Christian meeting. Here is one of the main aspects of ministry. Such teaching should be systematic and comprehensive, an aim which it is not easy to achieve with a plurality of teachers and preachers, but it should be possible for some scheme of teaching to be devised according to the needs of each local situation in which the various preachers would take part. The provision of a lectionary may be helpful in this regard, although it should not be assumed that a centrally devised lectionary is necessarily right for each individual congregation.

(b) Caring for the members. The pastoral care of the members stands alongside the ministry of teaching. It must be confessed that there is little directly on this topic in the New Testament, but the little that we do have suggests that pastoral care is primarily a spiritual matter. It is easy for pastoral care to be equated with a friendly call or the provision of some kind of

social care. While there is a proper place for the latter, it should be stressed that the spiritual element is the primary one and that it must not be forgotten. Unfortunately, we are in a situation where the idea of spiritual counsel is increasingly foreign, and people do not expect a conversation with a pastoral visitor to be concerned with their Christian life and experience. Gone are the days when the trembling visitee expected a spiritual catechism, and we can be thankful. But we have run to the other extreme, and the spiritual content of a pastoral visit or conversation is often low or nil.

(c) Assisting the needy. The care of the poor in the church, which was very important in the early church, may seem much less so today. But it is surely to be seen as the forerunner of the social welfare of today. The church has a responsibility for the social welfare of its members. In the contemporary British situation there is considerable secular provision of this kind, and the role of the church is proportionately reduced. Yet there is still an important place for such concern in the church, since the spiritual and social needs of the members are closely linked and the members of the church need a care which secular agencies cannot necessarily supply. Recognition of this fact, however, does not mean that Christian ministry is reducible to social care or that the primary task of ministry is at the social level. The story in Acts 6 stands as a reminder that prayer and the ministry of the word must not be endangered by social concern.

(d) Extending the church. A fourth area of ministry is evangelistic outreach. The missionary campaigns of Paul and his associates were seen initially as an extension of the work of the church in Antioch, a church which was engaged in proclaiming the gospel in its own immediate area, even if Paul became increasingly a freelance missionary and the churches which he founded were independent of that at Antioch. The outreach of the church was specifically evangelistic, in that it was intended to lead men and women to faith in Jesus Christ as Lord, and this should be a reminder to us that 'mission' means evangelism rather than, say, social outreach. Such mission will naturally be carried on by those who have the appropriate gifts of ministry.

5. Is There a Place for 'the Minister'?

These considerations naturally affect the question of the place of 'the minister' in the local church. Our point is that no one person should have a monopoly of ministerial functions but that these must be shared among all who are capable of exercising them. This can mean that in some situations 'the minister' becomes unnecessary, in the sense that the work of the church can carry on without him. But if a person with the training and experience of the traditional minister is available, clearly he can be of tremendous value in enabling the members of the church to accomplish their ministry more effectively. His role, therefore, is more that of a teacher and leader of ministers rather than that of a minister. He is primarily a *pastor pastorum*. If his role is not of the *esse* of the local church, it is of the *bene esse* of the local church; that is to say, he may not be essential, but he is desirable. He can occupy a position like that of Paul or Timothy or John the elder, there to give the church direct help as required, to help those who minister to do so more effectively, and to be available in situations of special need. One might sum up by saying that 'the minister's' job is to make himself dispensable – although it is unlikely that he will ever completely succeed in doing so!

Concluding Remarks

What has been said may raise a number of problems. First, the concept of ordination may seem to have become somewhat meaningless in the local situation. The difficulty arises from the fact that we have attached the New Testament practice of laying on of hands to one particular form of ministry which is not explicitly mentioned in the New Testament, 'the ministry of the word and sacraments'. But laying on of hands was used in New Testament times to appoint the seven appointed to look after poor relief in Jerusalem, to commission missionaries for a specific act of service (Acts 13.3), and to appoint a missionary like Timothy and possibly elders (I Tim. 5.22). This suggests that some kind of recognition and commissioning could be given to a wider group of persons. Those appointed to specific tasks in the local church could be formally installed through an appropriate form of service which might include the laying on of hands. There could be some difficulties in deciding how far to extend this practice, but these do not seem insuperable. It might, for example, be helpful to do something of this kind annually as a means of rededication.

Second, it may be asked whether we are in danger of forcing all members of the church to become busily involved in tasks of ministry. This has not been our intention. There is a priesthood of *all* believers, in the sense that all Christians are called personally into the service of God and can have the privilege of access to him without the need for any other intermediary than his son Jesus Christ. It is also true that in principle all Christians may have gifts of the Spirit to be used in ministry (I Cor. 12.7), but not all Christians may have specific gifts to be used in the congregation. There must be no suggestion that such people are in any way second-class citizens. Nor must we forget that the gifts of ministry are given to the church for the benefit of all its members. Each of us, whatever our own gifts may be, is to be helped by the gifts given to others. It would be false to have a church in which everybody is so busy ministering to other people that nobody is prepared to receive what others have to give them. If our stress in this essay has been on the active side of ministry, we must not forget that Jesus came to minister *to us*, and that our first priority as believers is to let him minister to us and serve us.

Finally, it needs to be emphasized that while our attention has focussed on questions of structure, the finest schemes of organization and even the strongest desire to be loyal to the teaching of the New Testament will do little to produce a new quality of ministry unless the vital element of the Spirit is present. Our claim is the more modest one that it is possible that our present style of ministry stifles the work of the Spirit. It could be that one way in which the Spirit will revitalize the church is by calling us to adopt a pattern of life which is more akin to that of the New Testament.

3

THE SACRAMENTS

Stephen Mosedale

Many Free Church buildings erected since the First World War follow the tradition in church architecture through the ages by having the communion table as the focus of attention. Often the pulpit looks like an afterthought. This is somewhat surprising, since in all these churches more time is spent gathered round the word than is spent gathered round the table. Yet a number of influences, notably the liturgical and ecumenical movements, have led to increased interest in the sacraments in churches which have previously given them less prominence. Evangelicals within such churches, probably from fear of precipitating the demise of preaching, have been slower than others to renew appreciation of the Lord's Supper, and instead have focussed attention on the baptism debate and its practical repercussions for ministry in the local church.

Nature and Spirit

Meanwhile, at local level it may be suspected that some Free Church people would feel little impoverishment if the sacraments were discontinued. A good number regard attendance at the Lord's Supper as a duty rather than as a privilege.[1]

Probably the chief modern intellectual barrier to being free to experience Christ in the sacraments is a misapprehension of the relationship of the material to the spiritual. Paul Tillich wrote, 'Nature has lost its religious meaning and is excluded from participation in the power of salvation; the sacraments have lost their spiritual power and are vanishing in the consciousness of many Protestants.'[2] The popular Christian response to the agnosticism and scepticism of the scientific age has been to avoid the dialogue of science and faith by separating the natural and spiritual realms. Zwingli's sentiment, though expressed for different reasons, finds modern echoes, 'Sensuous objects are irrelevant in the life of the Spirit. Faith, the sole requisite, needs no such external helps or assurances.'[3]

Now the religion of Jesus undoubtedly contained a corrective towards inward spirituality rather than outward ritual (John 4.24; Matt. 6.1–18; Luke 11.37–41; Mark 7.5, 6). Yet at the same time, through his parables, Jesus used the earthy business of everyday life to teach the deepest spiritual truths. And the incarnation itself gives to Christianity a unique appreciation of the part that both the material universe and the physical human body have to play in the scheme of salvation (Rom. 8.19–23; cf. I Thess. 5.23; Rev. 21.1).

In the created universe humankind has a place between animals and angels; unlike either we possess both body and soul. All our important activities, particularly personal relationships, have physical and spiritual dimensions. Perhaps love may sometimes begin as a mingling of spirit with spirit, but it dies quickly if it is not nourished through physical contact by means of speech, touch, movement, actions of service. There are also physical tokens shared in love relationships – things such as presents, kisses, handshakes, exchange of rings – which nobody would want to call 'mere symbols'. Since the Christian religion is a love affair we should joyfully accept the many and various material means of enriching it, the sacraments foremost among them.

More than Signs

While denying that the sacraments are either essential to salvation or a guarantee of it, it must be maintained that scripture does not view them as optional extras. Baptism is, along with repentance, the essential and immediate response to the gospel (Acts 2.38); later Peter states that 'baptism now saves you' (I Peter 3.21). Paul maintains that it is baptism that enables a person to share in the death and resurrection of Christ (Rom. 6.3, 4), and we can infer from I Cor. 10.14–24 that if idol feasts bond even the unbelieving participants to demons, then more surely does the Lord's Supper unite the believer with his Lord. In the light of such passages we should not hesitate to recognize the sacraments as effective means of grace, and to acknowledge the real presence of Christ in both.

Ministry and Liturgy

Before turning to the sacraments individually, two general matters concerning ministry in the local church require comment. The first is that the sacraments are the only part of the ministry of the local church which are normally the preserve of ordained ministers. In the Methodist Church, of which the present writer is a minister, the provisos whereby lay authorizations to preside at the Lord's Supper may be granted where ministerial manpower is overstretched,[4] and emergency baptism may be administered by 'any person present',[5] testify to belief that ordained ministers 'hold no priesthood differing in kind from that which is common to all the Lord's people and they have no exclusive title to the preaching of the gospel or the care of souls'.[6] Such affirmation of the priesthood of all believers finds more obvious expression in those denominations in which lay presidency at the Lord's Supper is much more common. If the trend continues towards more frequent celebration of this sacrament, perhaps in home groups as well as Sunday services, then some evangelicals would hope for a wider authorization of lay preachers and others to preside.

Philip was one of those appointed to table service rather than preaching (Acts 6.2–5), yet the impression is given that he baptized the first Samaritan and the first African Christians (Acts 8). Paul considered preaching to be a more important ministry for an apostle than baptizing (I Cor. 1.14–17). But present practice exalts the sacraments above the word, albeit unintentionally, so contributing to the notion that the minister possesses some unique charisma, with the result that ministers find it hard to persuade members to share in other forms of ministry.

Another way in which many Free Churches make the sacraments out of the ordinary is by forsaking their tradition of extempore prayer in favour of formal liturgy at the font or table.

Liturgy and free prayer can both be valuable in any kind of service, but by turning to the practice of using set forms for the sacraments we give many members the impression that these are something foreign to our Free Church ethos. Most people who say that they do not want more frequent communion services actually mean that they don't want to be bored by the same form of words week after week. While at the same time some in Methodism, for example, are urging that 'The Sunday Service' should be used even when the sacrament is not included,[7] the evangelical voice, aware that 'the letter kills, but the Spirit gives life', should commend at least as strongly the helpfulness of sometimes celebrating the Lord's Supper without any formal liturgy.

Baptism

1. The Meaning of the Water

It is generally agreed that the only essential part of the rite of baptism is that water should be sprinkled or poured on the person in the three-fold name (Matt. 28.19), and in cases of emergency this is deemed sufficient.[8] The meaning of baptism lies in the significance of the water. This point needs stressing, because so often in discussion the act of baptism is confused with the whole liturgy in which it takes place. The whole service, in the case of an adult who is being baptized (or indeed being confirmed subsequent to baptism in infancy), may rightly be described as a public declaration of faith or as entry into full church membership. The whole service at infant baptism (or indeed dedication) is a proclamation of prevenient grace, a dedication of the child to God and an opportunity for parents to commit themselves. But the water in baptism, the essential element, is neither a sign of grace nor a sign of faith. How does splashing a baby with cold uncomfortable water convey the love of God to anybody present? Or how is entering the baptistry a sign of faith when there is no real danger of drowning? Jesus was the master of the use of imagery, but if he intended the water of baptism to symbolize faith or grace he chose a rather obscure symbol.

It seems reasonable to suppose that Christian baptism was

instituted by Jesus on account of water's normal uses for drinking and washing, to preserve life and cleanliness. If I do not drink, I die. If I do not wash, I am soon unacceptable to other people. Spiritually too, without inward washing, the forgiveness of sin, I am unacceptable to God. Without drinking in, or being filled or baptized with, the Holy Spirit, the Life-giver, I am dead.

Nearly all the key Bible references to baptism refer to both forgiveness and the Holy Spirit. Ezekiel's promise of renewal involves sin-cleansing water and the gift of a new heart and spirit (Ezek. 36.25, 26). John's baptism was for the forgivensss of sins coupled with a promise of Holy Spirit baptism (Mark 1.4, 5, 8). When Jesus was baptized there was discussion concerning sinfulness and righteousness, and the descent of the Spirit on him (Matt. 3.13–17). At Pentecost forgiveness of sins and the gift of the Holy Spirit were the promised results of baptism (Acts 2.38). Paul reminds Titus, in the context of forsaking sin, that God 'saved us through the washing of rebirth and renewal by the Holy Spirit' (Titus 3.5). In other places also baptism is viewed either in terms of cleansing (e.g. Acts 22.16; Heb. 10.22; I Pet. 3.21) or in terms of baptism in the Spirit (e.g. Acts 1.5; 9.17, 18; 10.47; 19.5, 6; I Cor. 12.13; and possibly John 3.5).

So baptism is a sign and seal of the Spirit given and sins forgiven. It represents the change of life at conversion, the death of the old life of sin with resurrection to the new life in the Spirit, which is accomplished through union with Christ in his death and resurrection (Rom. 6.1–4; Col. 2.12). The World Council of Churches' Faith and Order Statement 'Baptism, Eucharist and Ministry', which many consider to be the most important ecumenical document produced for well over a millennium, summarizes the meaning of baptism by saying, 'Baptism is the sign of new life through Jesus Christ'.[9] Similarly, the statement of purpose in the Methodist service for infant baptism begins, 'The children of Christian parents are brought to be baptized with water as a sign of the new life in Christ'.[10]

2. Children of Christian Parents

If this understanding of baptism is right, then it is all those who possess the new life in Christ that should receive the sign in baptism. Nobody disputes that unbaptized adults should be baptized soon after conversion, but there is considerable controversy over three other groups: the children of Christians, the children of non-Christians and adults already baptized as babies. Should such be baptized on request? In considering this question it must be recognized that whilst the answers given here are considered to be biblical they are nevertheless personal opinions on what has been a major area of debate among evangelical Christians from pre-Reformation times. As others offer alternative insights from scripture it is vital that we seek to know the truth and do what is right in a spirit of love and mutual understanding.

Scripture appears to consider children as Christians along with their parents provided those parents live in faith. Such children, as they grow up, must, of course, affirm for themselves faith in Jesus to an increasing degree appropriate to their maturity. But in every area of life growing children gradually learn and experience independence, whilst at birth parents act totally on their children's behalf. In the vital matter of faith there is no reason to suppose it is otherwise.

Noah alone was worthy of salvation, yet God preserved his family with him: 'Go into the ark, you and your whole family, because I have found you (singular) righteous in this generation' (Gen. 7.1). (Interestingly, I Peter 3.20, 21 regards this salvation as symbolic of baptism.) This act of God provides the first biblical reference to his covenant (Gen. 6.18), and many of the subsequent Old Testament references to this covenant expressly mention the inclusion of children (See, e.g., Gen. 17.7; Deut. 5.2, 3; Ps. 103.17, 18; Isa. 59.21).

The New Testament does not conflict with this; indeed, Paul's message to the Philippian jailer closely parallels God's word to Noah, 'Believe (second person singular) in the Lord Jesus, and you will be saved – you and your household' (Acts 16.31). In the first Christian sermon Peter's appeal was, 'Be baptized . . . The promise is for you and your children' (Acts 2.38, 39). Christians married to unbelievers are encouraged to recognize that their children are 'holy' (I Cor. 7.14 – elsewhere the word is sometimes translated 'saints'), and elsewhere children and parents are addressed in the same breath as church members (Col. 3.20, 21; Eph. 6.1–4). Jesus said the kingdom belonged to little children and those who are like them (Matt. 19.14; 18.3). Against such a background it is reasonable to suppose the household baptisms (Acts 16.15; 16.33; I Cor. 1.16) included children, as did circumcision (Gen. 17.9–14), which seems to be regarded as parallel to Christian baptism (See Col. 2.11, 12).

Experience bears out this view in that those believers today who grew up in genuinely Christian homes can seldom recall a conversion experience. Like John the Baptist, who was less than the least in the kingdom of heaven (Matt. 11.11), they were filled with the Holy Spirit even from the womb, and were rightly baptized in infancy – immature Christians but more than just potential Christians.

This reading of scripture cannot support the view that children are justified and therefore fit subjects for baptism regardless of their parents' status with God. It is not denied that God's prevenient grace, his love for every person he has made, reaches out to every child and adult too. But, contrary to a very common approach which sees infant baptism as symbolizing this grace, and therefore unintentionally as quite a different sacrament from believers' baptism, it has been argued here that baptism is a sign of the whole change of life which can only take place where there is a response (personal, parental or corporate) to that grace. But even if theologically the case for infant baptism requires discrimination, it is sometimes argued that it is pastorally harmful to turn any parents away. In fact, evidence gathered recently by Neil Dixon[11] suggests that a rigorous policy carefully explained is more likely than a lax policy to lead to a family's conversion. The request of non-Christian parents for a baby's baptism should be seen, not as an opportunity to foster goodwill towards the church, but as an opportunity to make disciples for Christ. Anything, including the offer of a non-baptismal service of dedication or thanksgiving, which helps parents avoid the main issue of their own lack of commitment, and lends support to the belief that being a Christian means being baptized and trying to be good, is both a failure in evangelism and a failure to follow Christ, who allowed people to go away sad rather than accept them on their own terms (Luke 18.18–23; 9.57–62).

3. Rebaptism?

Many heartaches are caused and young Christians lost by churches which practise infant baptism, because it is the policy not to baptize as adult converts any known to have been once baptized in infancy.[12] The issues involved are complex, but hinge upon whether infant baptism is for every individual a valid equivalent to baptism as a believer. Quite clearly this point becomes a fit subject for debate if our theological justification for infant baptism differs from that for believer's baptism. On one interpretation of Acts 19.1–7 it may be argued that the disciples at Ephesus were rebaptized because an inadequate theology of baptism in regard to the Holy Spirit had accompanied their first baptism. Many share the view of the present writer, that if our practice and theology of infant baptism were revised along the lines already suggested, then requests for rebaptism would be fewer. Meanwhile the debate will no doubt continue as to whether rebaptism is ever permissible. One can appreciate the reluctance of the church to allow the validity of any sacrament to be questioned; but equally one can understand the viewpoint of some who feel that this involves too mechanical a view of the sacrament.

There will always be some in paedobaptist churches who reject infant baptism entirely. For we live in an age when the church has come to accommodate a wide variety of belief in regard to many doctrines, and people nowadays seldom choose their church on doctrinal grounds. The present writer considers it a welcome sign of the times that around the world today united churches find it possible to hold together two different understandings of who should be baptized, and dare to hope that one day they will be led into all the truth. Undoubtedly a reformation of the practice of apparently indiscriminate infant baptism will hasten the day when a bond of unity between paedobaptist and baptist churches will be possible, in which ministers of both convictions would jointly serve members of both convictions.

The Lord's Supper

1. The Meaning of the Bread and Wine

At his last meal with his apostles Jesus asked them to share bread and a cup as an *anamnēsis* of him (I Cor. 11.23–26; cf.

Matt. 26.26–29; Mark 14.22–25; Luke 22.15–20). 'Reminder' is a better translation than 'remembrance' or 'memorial' because we use it in a forward-looking as well as a backward-looking way, and Jesus spoke of the cup both as his blood poured out in death and as a foretaste of the new wine of the coming kingdom.

As with baptism, however, it is necessary to distinguish the meaning of the sacramental act of eating bread and wine from various ideas that have become associated with it during church history. For one thing, it is inadequate to describe the supper primarily as a thanksgiving or eucharist. Any meal, especially this one, is rightly treated as an occasion for thanksgiving (Matt. 26.26, 27; I Cor. 10.16; 11.24), and some meals are definite acts of celebration. Yet our normal eating of a meal is neither an act of thanksgiving or celebration, but one of nourishment. Again, we ought not to see the supper mainly in terms of communion or fellowship with one another, even though eating together is a precious and needed opportunity for that (Acts 2.44–46), and selfishness at the Lord's Supper in Corinth made the whole thing a tragic travesty (I Cor. 11.20–21). Some meals in daily life do have the express purpose of fostering friendship, as for example a reunion dinner, a lunch club, or a boy-girl supper date; but most meals are eaten primarily to satisfy hunger. It would seem also that to focus on the idea of the sacrament as a sacrifice of any kind leads away from the central meaning in terms of everyday eating and drinking for nourishment.

Daily food provides protein for growth, carbohydrate and fat for energy, and vitamins and minerals for health. As our bodies need food to stay alive, so too we die spiritually without the life-giving reality expressed by the sacrament. Now the gospel paradox is that such life is the fruit of death (John 12.23–25). The death of Jesus is life for us. The timing of the institution of the sacrament on the evening before his death, and at a Passover meal with its focus on God's ancient saving act accomplished through death, emphasizes this. So do the words 'my blood . . . poured out for many for the forgiveness of sins' (Matt. 26.28).

Lack of interest in the Lord's Supper is mainly due to a failure to get beyond the idea of its being a visual aid to help our 'remembrance' of the death of Jesus, to a discovery that like all food it has life-sustaining power. Earlier in his ministry, when Jesus spoke about eating his flesh and drinking his blood (John 6.35–58), he did not mention his death at all, he was making an offer of eternal life through feeding on him, the living bread from heaven, accompanied by a warning that without drinking his blood a person has no life or hope of resurrection. 'For my flesh is real food, and my blood is real drink. Whoever eats my flesh and drinks my blood remains in me, and I in him' (6.55, 56). When Jesus says the supper is his body and blood we must turn to this passage as the only explanation of what it means to eat and drink him: it is an interpretation in terms of nourishment, of staying alive.

So the Lord's Supper is the sign and seal of the essential gospel, the gospel of eternal life through remaining in Christ (e.g. John 16.1–7; 17.21–24). This is a theme developed in many ways through the New Testament; it is 'Christ in you, the hope of glory' (Col. 1.27). Again the WCC statement is clear about this: 'The Eucharist is essentially the sacrament of the gift which God makes to us in Christ through the power of the Holy Spirit. Every Christian receives this gift of salvation through communion in the body and blood of Christ . . . God himself acts giving life to the body of Christ and renewing each member.'[13]

2. Frequency of Celebration

We should want to celebrate the sacrament of Christ in us frequently, however we interpret the words 'whenever you drink' (I Cor. 11.25). The primitive church appears to have made their daily meal together a reminder of Jesus (Acts 2.42, 46), although it is possible that quite early a weekly gathering of the local church, including celebration of the 'breaking of bread', became the norm (Acts 20.7).

If the Lord's Supper really involves the heart of the gospel and is a means of grace, then we ought to hope for a weekly or at least fortnightly sharing of it in the course of regular worship. This would overcome the impression that it is a relatively unimportant addition to the normal routine of Christian and church life. Much progress has already been made by bringing the Lord's Supper into the main service in churches where previously it was tacked on at the end. My personal view is that if we were free to replace set prayers with extempore ones, to permit a wider use of lay people as presidents at the Lord's Supper, and to make a service with the Lord's Supper not much longer than a preaching service, then once members have been taught and convinced that the Lord's Supper is important, a weekly celebration is in sight.

3. An Open Table?

Many absent themselves from the Lord's table because they feel unworthy and because we are taught to examine ourselves before partaking to avoid being judged (I Cor. 11.27–32). In this passage Paul seems to have in mind the danger of treating the supper as a common meal without spiritual significance, but whatever his meaning he could not have intended to exclude Christians from the table, for by the same token they would be excluded from salvation, unworthy of the reality if unworthy of the sign.

All are unworthy. Such is the very ground of the invitation. Jesus did not come to call the righteous, but sinners (Mark 2.17). Conscious of unworthiness, but confident in faith, we should approach the table 'that our sinful bodies may be made clean by his body, and our souls washed through his most precious blood'.[14] Calvin criticized those who fenced the table, writing that 'it were too stupid, not to say idiotical, to require to the receiving of the sacrament a perfection which would render the sacrament vain and superfluous, because it was not instituted for the perfect, but for the infirm and weak'.[15] Today, ministers ought to make more of the opportunity the sacrament affords to contradict the false idea that Christianity is about trying to become worthy in the end of the reward of eternal life, and to proclaim instead the truth that God loved us while we were still sinners and gave us then the free gift of eternal life.

Because the gospel is medicine for the sick, and because the offer of grace is universal, it is right that the invitation to the Lord's table should be issued to all who seek Jesus, whether they are members of any church or none. In the present religious climate the question of the admission of adult non-members hardly arises, and instead discussion centres around the admission of baptized children to the Lord's Supper.

Theologically the practice of permitting children to receive the elements, as even infants do in the Orthodox tradition, is justified as the natural corollary of declaring them Christians by baptism. If the argument is sound for one sacrament then it is illogical not to accept it for the other. If our children possess the new life in Christ, then on what basis do we deny them the food Christ provides for their growth? If we issue an invitation 'to all who love Jesus', what right do we have to tell responding children that their love is not mature enough? If it is by faith that we enter the kingdom of heaven then we must remember that Jesus regarded the faith of little children as superior in quality to that of adults (Matt. 18.1–5; cf. 21.16). Children should share in the celebration of the Lord's Supper as part of their nurture in Christ, just as adults must. The act of blessing children, scriptural though it is (Mark 10.13–16), is a poor second best to letting them share fully in the sacrament. It courts the danger of ending up with the same kind of confusion that many church members have regarding baptism, namely that there is one sacrament for adults and another with a different meaning for children.

Perhaps much of the confusion in regard to both sacraments arises because, in our teaching, we address ourselves only to the great historical debates on questions no longer being asked. The contemporary attitude of many members to the sacraments can be summed up as 'I don't feel it makes any difference'. If that is the case there is one simple explanation for it. It must be that this is what their teachers, the ministers and other preachers, have conveyed to them, by our lack of teaching and our own lack of feeling. The great need today is for everyone entrusted with the ministry of teaching to explain simply and practically, on the basis of our understanding of the bible, why the sacraments do matter, and must not be treated with indifference.

Notes

1. The Methodist Church Basis of Membership, *Deed of Union* (1932), clause 33, states that it is a privilege and duty of members to avail themselves of the sacraments.

2. Paul Tillich, *The Protestant Era*, University of Chicago Press 1957, p. xxxviii.

3. Ulrich Zwingli, *True and False Religion*.

4. *The Constitutional Practice and Discipline of the Methodist Church*, Standing Order 011.

5. *The Methodist Service Book*, Methodist Publishing House 1975, p. A3, clause 14.

6. Op. cit., note 1, clause 30.

7. Op. cit., note 5, p. B18.

8. as note 5.

9. *Baptism, Eucharist and Ministry*, World Council of Churches, Geneva 1982, Baptism, para. 2.

10. Op. cit., note 5, p. A7, section 7.

11. Neil Dixon, *Troubled Waters*, Epworth Press 1979, pp. 132–140.

12. For this regulation in Methodism see op. cit., note 4, Standing Order 800.

13. Op. cit., note 9, Eucharist, para. 2.

14. Op. cit., note 5, p. B54, section 13.

15. John Calvin, *Institutes*, 4.XVII, para. 42.

4

WORSHIP

Peter W. Ensor

Worship is worth-ship. It is the ascribing to God that worth which is supremely his. It is 'giving God the glory due to his name'.[1] In the Bible the word 'worship' is used to translate a number of Greek and Hebrew terms, chief among which are the Hebrew root *shāhāh* and its Greek equivalent *proskuneo*, which basically mean 'bow down, prostrate oneself, make obeisance'. Sometimes, indeed, these two words are used of homage paid to men, but when used of homage paid to God they imply a kind of reverence and acknowledgment which uniquely belong to him.

Worship is of the utmost importance both in the life of the individual believer and also in the life of the local church. It is something for which God has made us. It is to be the eternal preoccupation of the redeemed people of God.[2] Indeed to 'glorify God and enjoy him for ever', as the Westminster divines so succinctly put it, is 'the chief end of man'.[3] Moreover true worship of God can be a source of great blessing. It is, according to William Temple, 'the quickening of conscience by his holiness; the nourishment of mind with his truth, the purifying of imagination by his beauty; the opening of the heart to his love; the surrender of will to his purpose . . . the way to the solution of perplexity and to the liberation from sin'.[4] In the last analysis, however, worship needs no utilitarian justification, nor is it to be engaged in primarily for the sake of its beneficial side-effects. It is an end in itself.

Worship is something for which we need to set aside time. While it is true that in biblical thought the ideas of 'worship' and 'service' are very closely related and that there is a sense in which the whole of the Christian life is to be an act of worship, the Bible also makes clear that we need to set aside time, both individually and corporately, when we can give God our whole attention. We must never, Martha-like, let our 'much serving' rob us of those times when we can simply 'sit at the Lord's feet' (Luke 10.38–42).

It is with the corporate worship of the local church that this chapter is concerned. Elements in that worship which are dealt with elsewhere in this book will not be covered in any detail here, but the aim will rather be to unearth the salient points of biblical teaching on the subject and then relate them to present day issues. There is much discussion nowadays about the forms our worship should take, and this must be part of our concern, but from the biblical perspective there are two other aspects of worship which are equally, if not more, important, and these must be dealt with first.

1. The Object of our Worship

The late Professor H. H. Rowley once said: 'the real meaning of worship derives in the first place from the God to whom it is directed'.[5] Since so much in our worship is determined by our conception of the character and being of God, it is imperative that this conception should be the right one. Worship is intimately related to theology.

The first two of the ten commandments are taken up with this issue. The first forbade the worship of any other gods but the Lord himself (Ex. 20.3; Deut. 5.7). In a day of widespread religious 'pluralism', the Israelites were told to maintain an exclusive allegiance to their God, and not to lapse into the idolatry of the surrounding nations,[6] something they did not always succeed in achieving. The second forbade the fabrication of any 'graven image, or any likeness of anything . . . ' for the purposes of worship, a prohibition which would have included images of the true God as well as of false gods (Ex. 20.4–6; Deut. 5.8–10).[7] The reason seems to be that any such image would fail to do justice to every aspect of God's character and would inevitably lead the worshipper to imagine the Lord to be something less than what he truly is. The greatness and incomparability of God, as the writer of Isaiah 40 saw so clearly, is such as to preclude the possibility of any adequate artistic representation (Isa. 40.18–24).

How then are we to conceive of the true God and so worship him aright? The Bible's own answer to this question is that we should conceive of God as he has revealed himself to be and worship him accordingly. The Israelites at Sinai saw no form; there was only 'a voice' (Deut. 4.12), and it was in response to that verbal self-communication of God that, in their better moments, they worshipped him. Time and again in scripture we find that the worship of God's people is prompted by some fresh message from God or some fresh manifestation of his glory.[8] Worship is response to revelation, man's *Antwort* to God's *Wort*.[9] Our own unaided imagination is likely to lead us astray, but if we pay attention to the ways in which God has revealed himself to us, then our worship will not be in vain.

It has been fashionable of late to locate the focal point of God's self-revelation almost entirely in the history of his people culminating in the life, death and resurrection of Jesus Christ. Evangelicals, however, have always maintained that God has revealed himself by means of the written testimony of scripture, which, they believe, accurately reports and correctly interprets the events of redemptive history. True worship will therefore, on this view, arise only when due attention has been paid to this source of information and our conception of the God we worship moulded by its teachings.

Let us briefly apply what has been said so far to three areas of topical importance:

(i) Does our worship today reflect a proper grasp of the greatness and majesty of the God of the Bible? I sense that the words spoken by A. W. Tozer a few decades ago are still true of many today: 'the Christian conception of God current in these middle years of the twentieth century is so decadent as to be wholly beneath the dignity of the Most High God and actually to constitute for professed believers something amounting to a moral calamity. With our loss of the sense of majesty has come the further loss of religious awe and consciousness of the divine presence. We have lost our spirit of worship and our ability to withdraw inwardly to meet God in adoring silence'.[10] Which is the God we adore? A soft, grandfatherly figure who exists largely to look after us, or a God who is not only 'love' but also 'light' and 'a consuming fire' (I John 4.8; 1.5; Heb. 12.29), who not only forgives, but also judges, who not only offers all, but also demands all? Is our conception of God based merely on a few favourite New Testament passages, or on the totality of the Bible revelation?

(ii) We are living in an ever-increasingly 'pluralistic' society ourselves. The immigrant population has aided the spread of non-Christian faiths. Our attitude to these faiths is having to be more clearly defined and the question of the validity of inter-faith worship is being asked. What is to be our reply? Love for our neighbours should clearly move us to tolerate, respect, listen to, learn from and engage in 'dialogue' with adherents of other faiths. Bridges of mutual understanding should be built and we must be ready to appreciate the extent to which the Christian understanding of God overlaps that of other faiths. However, the biblical Christian will not feel able to sacrifice the uniqueness of the Christian revelation, and of Christ in particular,[11] in some form of syncretistic compromise. He will still seek to bring people to Christ, people of other faiths as well as those of none, and will still believe that only in Christ may true, spiritual unity between the nations be found.[12] He will not therefore be happy with any worship that is overtly syncretistic, such as that proposed by the World Congress of Faiths,[13] nor indeed with any kind of lowest-common-denominator type of worship which fails to give Christ the honour which is his due, simply because it fails to do justice to God's total self-revelation.

(iii) We are also living in days when the traditional trinitarian understanding of God is very much under attack, largely through reductionist estimates of the person of Christ. I believe that *The Myth of God Incarnate*[14] was one example of this trend. It should not be forgotten that this issue has important implications for worship. If the scholars who wrote *The Myth* are right, then, as Athanasius argued against Arius long ago, the worship of Jesus is idolatrous, since it would be the worship of a creature rather than of one who was himself God.[15] Our hymnody, for one thing, would have to be radically revised. If however, the traditional understanding may still be held to be consistent with scripture, as I believe it may, then the worship of the Triune God, Father, Son and Holy Spirit, will not only continue to be permissible, but will also be the most fitting way of responding to the revelation God has given us of himself.

2. *The Reality of our Worship*

It is interesting to note that in the recorded teaching of Jesus on the subject of worship, it was this aspect of it that was his primary concern; not the external characteristics of worship such as its structure and form, but rather its internal character- istics, its reality, authenticity, depth.

Take, for example, the record of Jesus' conversation with the woman at the well in Sychar, to be found in John 4. At verse 20 the woman introduces what is probably a 'red herring' to avoid Jesus' probing into her private life: 'our fathers worshipped on this mountain; and you say that in Jerusalem is the place where men ought to worship'. But Jesus turns the digression to good advantage by showing that the kind of worship God now desires is not to be determined by any particular location, but only by his own nature: 'God is spirit and those who worship him must worship in spirit and truth' (John 4.24). Even in Old Testa- ment days the formal worship centred on the temple at Jerusalem was intended to be but the vehicle for the inner devotion of the worshipper.[16] Now that Jesus had come, and the old forms were soon to be made obsolete, God's intentions for the nature of our worship were to become clearer still. God desires worship that is spiritual, that engages the whole of our being and that brings us into genuine contact with himself. Unless our worship is of this quality then, whatever forms we may use, it is in vain that we worship him.

Similarly in Mark 7, with its parallel in Matthew 15, we find Jesus insisting on the necessity of the inner kind of devotion in the context of a debate with the Pharisees over the relatively trivial matter of washing one's hands before a meal. Jesus goes straight to the heart of the issue with a quotation from Isaiah 29.13: 'this people honours me with their lips, but their heart is far from me; in vain do they worship me, teaching as doctrines the precepts of men' (Mark 7.6, 7; Matt. 15.8, 9). The Pharisees' concern about keeping the 'tradition of the elders' was merely a symptom of a deeper malaise: mere externalism in religion in general and in worship in particular. The Pharisees loved to 'stand and pray in the synagogues and at the street corners, that they may be seen by man' (Matt. 6.5; cf. Luke 18.9–14 for parabolic illustration). Such lip-worship was in vain, for God desires that we should worship him with our hearts as well.

What is the 'heart'? In Hebrew thought the words *lēbāb* and *lēb* were in the main used to describe what may be called the 'inner man', the seat of the mind, the will, and the emotions, and it is in this sense that we are to understand the meaning of the 'heart' in Mark 7. Heart worship will therefore involve the three constituent parts of our psychological make-up as enumerated above. Let us see how this works out in practice: (i) Heart-worship involves the mind. Our mental capacities are to be in full use in worship. We are to love the Lord our God with all our minds (Matt. 22.37; Mark 12.30; Luke 10.27). God is not pleased with mindless devotion. We must listen carefully to the scriptures as they are read and expounded, discipline our minds to concentrate on the words of the hymns we sing and of the prayers we pray, and open them to receive the truth God wants to share with us. Even if we engage in periods of corporate silence such as are advocated by some traditions within the church, or, to go to the other extreme, in the kind of corporate 'singing in tongues' to be found in charismatic circles today, our minds are still not to be blank, but rather concentrated on the Lord we seek to adore. (ii) Heart-worship involves the will. As Paul says at one point real worship includes the presenting of our 'bodies as a living sacrifice, holy and acceptable to God' (Rom. 12.1). We cannot truly worship God unless we are willing at the same time to lay all 'on the altar', to give ourselves unreservedly to him, and allow him to do with us whatever he wants. Time and again the Old Testament prophets were moved to upbraid their contemporaries because of their failure at this very point, because worship was not accompanied by holy living.[17] If our worship on Sundays makes no difference to the way we behave for the remainder of the week then it is in vain. (iii) Heart-worship involves the emotions. If the gospel affects the whole man, and emotions are part of the whole man, then the gospel affects the emotions. Of course we must be wary of emotionalism and loss of emotional self-control, but we must also be wary of a purely cerebral form of Christianity. In the Bible, people seem to have been less inhibited in the expression of their emotions in worship than we are today; they could weep as they did in Nehemiah's day 'when they heard the words of the Law' (Neh. 8.9) or they could dance for joy, as David did when he brought the ark of the Lord into Jerusalem (II Sam. 6.14; cf. Ps. 149.3; 150.4). While it is true that the extent to which we give expression to our emotions will depend largely on our individual temperaments and social setting, we must not despise such expression when it occurs. Its presence is rather a sign that worship is emanating not just from the 'top of our heads' but also from the 'bottom of our hearts'.

Such is the worship that God desires, but how may it be ours? If we are honest, too much of our worship is lip-worship, a mechanical repetition of forms with which we have been long familiar which lacks the kind of reality and depth Jesus emphasized as necessary. The New Testament answer points us to the person and work of the Holy Spirit. It is he who helps us to 'understand the gifts bestowed on us by God', who helps us through Christ to have 'access to the Father', who assures us of our filial relationship to him, who enables us to pray as we ought, who inspires the various gifts and ministries of the members of the body of Christ, and who moves us to worship 'in psalms and hymns and spiritual songs, singing and making melody to the Lord with all the heart' as we let our lives be filled with his presence and power (I Cor. 2.12; Eph. 2.18; Rom. 8.15, 16, 26; I Cor. 12; Eph. 5.18, 19). If our worship is to be heart-worship, worship in spirit and in truth, real worship, then we must seek a greater openness to the renewing power of the Holy Spirit in our lives.

3. The Forms our Worship Should Take

We have seen that we should worship God according to his own self-revelation, and that we should worship him in spirit and in truth. But what should actually happen when the local church gathers together to worship him week by week? What guidance do the scriptures give us here?

Our answer must be that while they do indeed give us direction in this matter by way of basic principles and descriptions of the practices of the earliest churches, they give us very little in the way of detailed prescriptions. We find here no blueprints, no stereotypes, no specific instructions of the kind we find, for example, in the sub-apostolic *Didache* or later manuals of church discipline. Within the broad principles governing Christian worship which may be derived from the biblical material, much room seems to be left for variety, adaptation and flexibility.

This is in itself an important fact to bear in mind as we seek to order worship for today. If the Bible gives us such freedom, then we are not bound as by some divine law to the traditional practices of the church at any age or place, whether it be eighteenth- or nineteenth-century English Methodism, or that 'golden age' of some liturgiologists – the age of the early church fathers, or any other. We are not necessarily to worship in a certain way simply because we have always done it that way, nor are we to idolize any particular period of church history as being the ideal to which everybody else must conform. For example, to advocate weekly communion, rigid adherence to the lectionary, the placing of the intercessions after the sermon is one thing; to insist on them as though they were part of some universal divine law is another. Similarly with the advocacy of free prayer to the exclusion of set prayer, or 'spontaneous' worship to the exclusion of 'structured' worship. The Holy Spirit may indeed lead us in one particular direction in these matters, but we should not discount the possibility that he may be leading others in another.

Granted, then, that the Bible gives us no blueprint for the form of our worship, what guidance does it give? Perhaps five principles may be singled out as being among the most important:

(i) There must be a proper balance between our speaking to God and God's speaking to us. Worship should serve to deepen our relationship with God, and, as with any relationship, two-way communication is essential. Both elements were present in biblical worship, to a greater or lesser degree. They were present in the Old Testament cultus, where priests (representing the people's approach to God) and prophets (representing God's approach to the people) played their distinctive and complementary roles. They were present in the worship of the synagogue, in which the reading, translating and exposition of the sacred writings were complemented by praise and prayer. They were also present in the worship of the earliest Christians who 'devoted themselves' both to 'the apostles' teaching' and also to 'the prayers' (Acts 2.42). Both elements should be given their proper weight today. God's speaking to us may be expressed through scripture reading, sermon, or sacrament; it may also be expressed through drama, dialogue or other experimental forms, provided they actually communicate something from God and do not merely raise questions or create unresolved problems. Our speaking to God may be expressed through hymns and prayers, which must be allowed to express a variety of responses, whether of adoration, thanksgiving, confession, supplication, intercession or dedication. Whatever forms these basic ingredients take, and however they are ordered within a service, there must be this sense of two-way communication between ourselves and God, and an awareness at the end that we have met with him.

(ii) There must be a proper balance between form and freedom, or between what may be described as 'liturgical' and 'charismatic' elements in public worship. Once again we see these elements in biblical worship at its best, although it seems that in times of spiritual declension the 'charismatic' element tended to die away and leave behind an arid formalism. It is interesting to see how the two elements were allowed for in the worship of the New Testament church in particular. We find on the one hand a readiness to participate in the relatively stereotyped worship of the temple[18] and the synagogue[19] (a readiness that had been shared by Jesus himself),[20] and also evidence for the use of certain set formulae which would have been used in the context of specifically Christian worship.[21] On the other hand, however, we also find among Christians a degree of freedom and spontaneity of expression unparalleled in the worship of their Jewish contemporaries. One thinks of the impromptu prayer meetings recorded in the book of Acts,[22] the spontaneous outbursts of praise as whole groups were filled with the Holy Spirit,[23] and, most notably of all, the exercise of 'charismatic' gifts in the regular worship of the early local church.[24]

Both elements are needed today. There is nothing wrong with formal liturgies. Those who oppose them often forget that our hymns and our constant reiteration of the Lord's Prayer fall into the same category. Though indeed there are the dangers of aridity, staleness and unreality if they are used to excess, they may still be the vehicle of true, spiritual worship and can serve to enhance worship by providing a backcloth of objectivity, dignity and catholicity. At the same time, however, there is nothing wrong with 'charismatic' worship either, worship in which both leader and congregation come more immediately under the direction of the Holy Spirit, feel free to pray as they are led by him, and exercise whatever gifts they may have been given by him. Once again there are dangers here both of '*de facto*' formalism on the one hand, and loss of 'decency and order' on the other,[25] but at its best this kind of worship can bring in a freshness and vitality which can help all those present to come into living contact with the living God.

How, and to what extent, this principle of worship may be actually implemented in any one place will depend largely on local conditions, but we must hold the ideal before our eyes, and seek a balance which is both scriptural and satisfying.

(iii) Worship must be a truly corporate affair. Once again, the church of the New Testament shows us the way. Not only do the images believers used to describe themselves – such as that of the 'body of Christ'[26] – express this sense of corporate solidarity, but also the evidence suggests that in worship, in particular, there was a greater degree of participation on the part of each of the members of the body than is common today. They did not come together to watch a 'one man show' – as our present situation has been caricatured – but actively to share themselves in the corporate worship of the local church. 'When you come together, each one has a hymn, a lesson, a revelation, a tongue or an interpretation . . . ' says Paul (I Cor. 14.26) in an approving tone, and his problem in this area was not with the reluctant but with the over-enthusiastic!

In recent years both the 'liturgical' and the 'charismatic' movements have, in their different ways, been seeking to implement this principle. True, where a meeting is more evangelistic in thrust, it is only right that the centre of gravity should shift to the element of proclamation, and therefore to the preacher himself, but where a meeting is geared rather to the edification of the local church, then this idea of congregational participation should be allowed to operate. Once again, local conditions will determine to a large extent how it will work out in practice.

A further way in which this principle may be applied, especially in churches with large congregations, is through the creation of mid-week fellowship groups. These give the opportunity for members of the local church to relate to one another at greater depth, and also, in the context of the Bible study, praise and prayer, opportunity to share these insights and use those gifts which God has given them as well as to receive from others in a way which perhaps is not possible in Sunday worship. This leads us straight on to our fourth principle.

(iv) Worship must serve to edify the church. It is interesting to note how often Paul brings this principle to bear upon his discussion of Christian worship in I Corinthians 12–14. To Christians who were tending to be exhibitionist in their use of spiritual gifts, he reminds them that the manifestation of the Spirit has been given 'for the common good' (I Cor. 12.7). To those who were prone to engage in a spate of uninterpreted tongues-speaking, he reminds them of the greater value of intelligible speech, which can give 'upbuilding and encouragement and consolation' (I Cor. 14.3; cf. 14.4, 5, 12, 19, 26) to those present. Edification is therefore a further principle that should govern our worship today. Are we strengthened and renewed in our Christian faith as a result of our worship? Are we brought closer to God? Are we better equipped to serve him in the world? It was this principle, for example, that moved the Reformers to urge the use of the vernacular language in worship instead of the outmoded Latin. It should move us today to ensure that our language too is simple, straightforward and clear, our message relevant to the needs of the congregation, and the whole conduct of our worship a means of blessing to those who participate in it.

(v) Finally, our worship must bring glory to God. We end where we began. However much worship may and must edify God's people, this is ultimately a by-product of something which is intrinsically worthwhile in itself, namely, that glorification of God for which we were made. We have been 'destined and appointed to live for the praise of his glory' (Eph. 1.12). We are together 'with one voice' to 'glorify the God and Father of our Lord Jesus Christ' (Rom. 15.6). We are to use whatever gifts we may have been given 'in order that in everything God may be glorified through Jesus Christ' (I Peter 4.11). The acme of worship is attained when we can echo the worship of the hosts of heaven and say 'to him who sits upon the throne and to the Lamb be blessing and honour and glory and might for ever and ever!' (Rev. 5.13). There should be no self-display or self-projection on the part of those leading worship, nor should worship degenerate into a form of spiritual entertainment or a series of gimmicks, for all these things tend to obscure the glory of God and to cheapen the inestimable and awesome privilege we have of communion with him. In the end, our aim should be simply to see him with the eyes of faith, and seeing him to be 'lost in wonder, love and praise'.

Notes

1. *The Senior Catechism of the Methodist Church*, question 47.
2. Cf. Rev. 4.5; 11.15–19; 15.2–4; 19.1–10; 22.1–5.
3. *Westminster Confession Shorter Catechism*, question 1.
4. W. Temple, *Readings in Saint John's Gospel*, Macmillan, 1940, p. 68.
5. H. H. Rowley, *Worship in Ancient Israel: its Forms and Meaning*, SPCK, 1976, p. 251.
6. Cf. also Ex. 23.23, 24; 34.14; Deut. 4.19; 8.19; 11.16; 17.2–7; Josh. 23.6–8; I Kings 9.6, 7; II Kings 17.34–40; Psalm 81.9.
7. Cf. also Lev. 26.1; Deut. 4.15–19; Rom. 1.22–25.
8. E.g. Ex. 4.31; 12.21–27; 34.5–8; Judg. 7.15; Neh. 9.3; cf. also John 9.35–38; Rev. 1.12–17.
9. Cf. R. Abba, *Principles of Christian Worship*, Oxford University Press, 1957, p. 45.
10. A. W. Tozer, *The Knowledge of the Holy*, J. Clarke, 1965.
11. Cf., e.g., John 14.6; Acts 4.12; I Tim. 2.5.
12. Cf., e.g., Eph. 1.9, 10; 2.11–22.
13. Cf. P. R. Akehurst and R. W. F. Wootton, *Inter-faith Worship*, Grove Books, No. 52, 1977, pp. 17, 18.
14. John Hick (ed.) *The Myth of God Incarnate*, SCM Press 1977.
15. That Jesus was worshipped in the New Testament church – itself evidence of their incipient belief in his full deity – is shown by, e.g., R. P. Martin, *Worship in the Early Church*, Marshall, Morgan and Scott, 1964, pp. 31–33.
16. Cf. H. H. Rowley, op. cit., ch. 4.
17. E.g. Isa. 1.12–17; Jer. 7.9, 10; Amos 5.21–24; Micah 3.4; 6.6–8.
18. E.g. Luke 24.53; Acts 2.46; 3.1; 21.23–26; 22.17.
19. E.g. Acts 6.9; 9.20; 13.5, 14; 14.1, 17.1–4; 18.4, 19, 26; 19.8.
20. E.g. John 2.13–17; 5.1; 7.10; 18.20; Luke 4.16–21; Matt. 4.23; Mark 1.39.
21. For this evidence cf. R. P. Martin, op. cit., chs 3–5; O. Cullman, *Early Christian Worship*, SCM Press 1953; C. F. D. Moule, *Worship in the New Testament*, Grove Books 1978, ch. 5.
22. E.g. Acts 4.24–31; 12.12; 16.25.
23. E.g. Acts 2.4, 11, 17, 18; 10.46; 19.6.
24. E.g. Rom. 12.6–8; I Cor. 12–14; Eph. 4.11.
25. Cf. I Cor. 14.40.
26. E.g. Rom. 12.4, 5; I Cor. 12.27; Col. 2.19; 3.15; Eph. 2.16; 3.6; 4.4, 16; 5.23, 30.

5

PREACHING

John Horner

Preaching Today

The effectiveness of the average Free Church Sunday service still depends largely upon the quality of the sermon. To be sure, the day has gone when 'princes of the pulpit' were able to draw large and enthusiastic audiences, and though some preachers can still attract crowds, they do so these days not because of their pulpit eloquence and expertise, but because of highly successful and widely publicized ministries in their own churches or organizations. But though it is unlikely that any church today will be filled solely by preaching brilliance, it is a fact that a church can be emptied, or at least reduced to a minimum of the faithful, by inadequate preaching. The local minister may be a caring pastor or an able administrator; the service may regularly include a reverent and sensitive celebration of Holy Communion; but unless that church has a programme of weekday activities exceptionally well integrated into Sunday worship, it is unlikely that attendance at the Sunday worship will increase if the preaching is consistently dull and unhelpful.

It is not surprising to learn from a recent survey of church attendance in Cornwall[1] – a county perhaps more exposed than any other English county to Methodist preachers – that one of the main reasons for the dramatic decline in church-going is given as 'long and boring sermons'. But whereas many may be lost to the church by 'foolish' preaching, it still pleases God to save by 'the foolishness of preaching' (I Cor. 1.21), which is not the same thing at all. The 'foolishness of preaching' is the proclamation of the saving act of God in and through Christ and him crucified (I Cor. 1.17–31). Where that truth in its various aspects is faithfully and imaginatively proclaimed there is usually no shortage of hearers.

Good preaching contains many elements which combine to give the sermon its place of unique importance in the service. It is a means of teaching the doctrines of the church, of explaining its symbols, rituals and practices, of unifying and directing church members within one strategy and purpose, of instructing in moral issues and suggesting guide-lines for conduct, of stimulating and encouraging social concern and action, of reassuring the weak and reproving the proud, and of communicating the love, power and peace of God in Christ. More than words, it should and may be a joyous, challenging, exciting experience. Music, drama, dialogue, discussion, rituals and liturgies may all have their contribution to make to worship, but they cannot take the place of the preaching.

Difficulties for the Evangelical Preacher

Surveys analysing the reasons for church growth – and they are becoming almost as numerous as those of the 1950s and 60s analysing church decline – reveal that one factor common to growing churches is Bible-based preaching. Here some preachers may have a problem – the problem of preaching a biblical message in a church not wholly committed to biblical principles and practices. We shall consider some of the areas in which this conflict emerges.

The preacher who is faithful to scripture may find himself preaching a gospel of salvation by faith in a church which assumes that it will be justified by works. A 'live' church to such is the same thing as a busy one – a church where there are lots of things going on, irrespective of what sort of things they are. At the personal level, moral rectitude and good neighbourliness are considered to be the sole qualifications for salvation. Or he may find himself preaching the importance of quality in a church given to make evaluations in terms of quantity. A concert attracting two hundred people will be seen to have more significance than a prayer meeting attended by three. The answer to the question, 'How are things at your church these

days?' will probably be given in terms of the size of the
congregations and collections.

He may find himself preaching a message of revival in a
church concerned only with survival. Many churches are
victims of that dreadful downward spiral of working desperately to keep the doors open in order that others may come and
help them to work desperately to keep the doors open in order
that . . . and so on. Or he may find himself preaching a message
of trusting to a church which at best is trying. So many
churches have not grasped the fact that we are not in business to
build the kingdom. The kingdom is a gift. We are to *receive* it
(Luke 12.32). And the qualities needed to make it possible for a
church to receive this gift are themselves gifts (Rom. 12.6–8;
Eph. 4.7–13; I Cor. 12.7–11).

He may find himself preaching entry into the family of God
by the new birth (John 1.12, 13; 3.3–7; Rom. 8.14–17) in a
church which teaches that we are received into God's family at
our baptism.[2] Or he may find himself preaching the priesthood
of all believers in a church which gives exclusive rights to a
priestly caste – its ministers. He might even find himself trying
to be obedient himself and urging others to be obedient to
Christ's twin commission to preach and heal (Matt. 10.1, 7, 8;
Mark 6.12, 13; Luke 9.2; 10.9) in a church which has given no
thought at all to non-physical means of healing.

He may find himself commending a church which is an
organic community, flexible, sensitive to person-to-person and
Spirit-to-person encounters and allowing for a high degree of
spontaneity, in a church which is obliged to maintain its
existence within the inflexible structure of 988 standing orders!

So what is he to do? If the preacher belongs to a church which
does not practise what he preaches, he must either (a) join
another church where his preaching and the practice of the
church are consistent – a step taken by many as is shown by the
transfer-growth statistics of the house church movement;
(b) preach what his church practises, thereby being disloyal to
what for him may be important principles; or (c) go on
preaching biblical principles even though they are in conflict
with what his church practises.

It is the adoption of this latter compromise that has done so
much to weaken the effectiveness of the Bible-based sermon.

Preaching unrelated to practice – often indeed in conflict with it – becomes remote, irrelevant and 'unreal'. It cannot be related to the life of the church as it is. It cannot be adopted and woven into the strategy and mission of the church in which it is preached. And so the preacher is regarded at best as misguided; at worst, a crank.

More will be said later about the relation of the sermon to the hearer. Before coming to that, however, we shall examine more closely this Bible-based preaching to which we have been referring. We shall do so under two heads: 'Why Expository Preaching?' and 'Preparing the Expository Sermon.'

Why Expository Preaching?

The answer to this question is not because surveys show that Bible-based ministers preach to growing churches, but because the expository preacher is sharing with his hearer the word of God as revealed in scripture. Why is this a good thing to do?

1. Because People Need It

The unsaved must be presented with the challenge and offer of God in Christ as revealed in the Bible. And the saved, if they are to grow in grace, wisdom and holiness, must be fed from the word of God as we have it in the Bible. Many churches have no regular weeknight meeting at which there is systematic Bible teaching. And in churches where there are such meetings it is probably true to say that most of the members of the congregation do not go to them. All the more important then that a Bible-based message should be preached on Sundays.

2. Because People Welcome and Respond to It

To good expository preaching, that is. Not to a string of vaguely related biblical verses. 'He took us all through the Bible from Genesis to Revelation' is a comment sometimes heard of preachers. And the words are not spoken in appreciation, but with the tired despair of those who have been taken on a long wearisome journey and have arrived nowhere. But let a preacher expound the scripture with conviction, warmth and clarity and the hearers will acknowledge with a joy, sometimes laced with surprise, the relevance and authority of the word.

3. Because God Blesses It

That same life-giving Spirit which inspired God's word in the original scripture, quickens good exposition. The word of the preacher comes alive with power. It reaches mind, soul and spirit. It is endued with a compelling quality that is more than the power of language, more than the persuasiveness of eloquence, more than the compulsion of argument.

The Expository Sermon

We shall now consider the composition and characteristics of the expository sermon.

1. Choosing the Passage for Exposition

Clearly the first thing to do when preparing an expository sermon is to find a suitable passage for exposition. How is this to be done? Ideally, perhaps, the passage should 'find' the preacher. It should, as it were, leap at him out of the page of scripture and demand to be expounded. And it should give him no rest until he has surrendered to its demand. Many of us have known that experience. But we know too that such moments tend not to come often enough to stimulate a supply of sermons equal to the weekly demand. So other ways of finding a suitable passage must be sought.

Do not despise the lectionary. There are some preachers who believe that unless their message is 'given' spontaneously by God and developed without forethought under the immediate guidance of the Holy Spirit, it is not truly of God. This is to take too limited a view of the power and inspiration of the Holy Spirit and the nature of God's anointing. The fact that the passage for exposition comes from a section of the Bible selected months previously by people unknown to the preacher and unfamiliar with the circumstances of the church in which it is to be preached, does not necessarily mean that the exposition has no chance of receiving the blessing of God or of being relevant to local needs. Whatever the passage may be, it is a word of God. There will be some truth in it for both preacher and congregation.

Successive expositions of extended passages from the Bible

can be prepared; for example, the Lord's Prayer, the Beatitudes, the Sermon on the Mount or one of the shorter epistles in its entirety. Of course, this is only practicable where the preacher is in the same pulpit fairly often. The rural minister who has pastoral oversight of a number of churches or chapels will take a long time to preach a verse-by-verse exposition of the Sermon on the Mount!

The length of a passage for exposition may vary considerably from a fairly short statement to an exposition of a whole parable or discourse. But a very short statement – 'God is love' for instance – treated out of context could hardly be considered sufficient material for an expository sermon; while a lengthy passage might lend itself more to a Bible-study than to a sermon. The passage chosen should be short enough not to confuse the hearers with too much information, and long enough to do justice to the word in its context.

2. *The Passage Considered in the Light of Experience*

Before turning to the commentaries, it is a good thing to meditate prayerfully upon the passage chosen for exposition in the light of one's own experience and of what one knows about the needs of the people who are to receive the exposition. This can be done by asking questions like, 'What is God saying to me now through this passage?' 'What has he already said to me through this passage?' 'Can I testify to the truth of this from my own experience?' 'In what ways?' It is always helpful if a preacher can relate his own experience to the exposition. It gives his preaching an added authority by rooting it in the reality of something that actually happened. But it is not essential. We are in the pulpit to declare what God has promised and done, not what we have proved and experienced.

Questions relating to the hearers might be, 'Who are the people who are going to hear this sermon?' 'What are their basic needs?' 'What are their special needs?' 'Is encouragement appropriate? Or reproof?' 'Has anything happened recently in the life of the congregation which could make this passage particularly relevant?' This whole business of relating the message to the specific needs and opportunities of the hearers is so important that further reference will be made to it in an exploration of a 'shared' ministry of the word.

3. The Value of the Commentaries

When the passage has been chosen, and considered in the light of the preacher's experience and the needs of his hearers, then it is time for the preacher to avail himself of the learning and insights of the biblical scholars. It is probably better to do it in this order – that is, personal reflection before the commentaries – because it would seem important to focus right from the start on the personal and local relevance of the message, before a commentary sets the mind off on some interesting line of thought which could prevent one from ever discovering the main thrust of the passage as it should be applied to the receiving congregation. Once that main thrust has been found, material from the commentaries may be used to sharpen, apply or illuminate it.

Though modern versions are a great help in the understanding of the Bible, commentaries can give insights and understandings which translations cannot. Words have overtones and associations which translations cannot always bring out. Commentaries can give useful background information relating to the thinking or customs of the time which help in the understanding of the passage. Also parallels with or contrasts to passages elsewhere in the Bible will be indicated in a good commentary and will be helpful to the expositor.

It should be admitted that reading the commentary after one has done one's own reflection on a passage can sometimes be a rather devastating experience. It can show just how much one's own thinking and interpretation were mistaken. In this event, the preacher must be prepared to surrender to the facts. The chances are that if he has come to some mistaken interpretation of the scripture, others may have done so too. So it might not be out of place to acknowledge this in the sermon itself perhaps in the form of some parting gesture like, 'I wonder if you thought as I did that this passage meant . . . when in fact I learn that it means . . .'

4. The Importance of Structure

Many preachers seem reluctant or unable to structure their sermons, though to do so is of enormous help to the hearer. It helps him to see where he is going. And it helps him to see where he has been. The old-fashioned three-point sermon has a lot to commend it. Most people can remember three points clearly expressed, and there is a satisfying balance in the beginning/middle/end structure. As Spurgeon once said, 'A three-legged stool will sit firm on any surface.' Sometimes, of course, an exposition will naturally follow an unfolding line of argument and will not submit easily to a structured form. So be it. On no account must the truth be distorted for the sake of structure. The temptation to do this is particularly acute when we are looking for alliterative section headings.

5. *Avoiding Dullness*

As has been noted above, people have stopped going to church because they have been bored by sermons, not because they have been offended by them. We preachers have managed, God forgive us, to turn the joyous and exhilarating religion of Jesus into something dull. It's not that there is anything new to be said. Almost the last words of the Bible are a warning of the consequences of adding to the word of God (Rev. 22.18). But we must find new ways of presenting old truths so that our hearers will prick up their ears with keen attention and say to us afterwards, 'I'd never thought about it like that before.' How then are we to avoid dullness in our preaching? There are several ways. One is by not labouring the obvious. One woman said of her minister, 'He spends his time in the pulpit laboriously making the obvious sound profound.' It may, of course, be necessary to state the obvious in order to give the whole truth. But some sermons are no more than a series of scripture passages amplified into boringly obvious re-statements. In others, platitudes, clichés and commonplaces abound inducing a deadly state of torpor in the minds of the hearers. On the other hand, the preacher should avoid putting on a display of homiletical or verbal acrobatics in which the truth is presented in every pose except the upright! Too much brilliance dazzles and blinds rather than illuminates. So, though congregations must not be subjected to boredom through over-exposure to the obvious, the preacher must be prepared to accept the fact that at the end of the day it may well be not his fascinating new insight into the truth that he will be thanked for, but some platitude related to the theme of the sermon as a whole and which he assiduously avoided!

We can also guard against dullness by avoiding the predictable. I well remember one long-suffering church steward who
had listened to two sermons every Sunday for 60 years (over
6000 sermons!) saying to me, 'With most preachers, the
moment they announce their text, you know just what they are
going to say. There is a sermon on faith, and a sermon on
salvation, and a sermon on love and a few others and I've heard
them preached scores of times by scores of preachers.' This
challenge of not stating the predictable is related to the previous
one of avoiding the obvious. To meet this challenge it will not
help to choose obscure subjects and weird unheard-of texts and
to spend one's preaching days forever on the unfamiliar
peripheries of the Christian life. Christ's people must be kept
generally at the centre of the truth. Perhaps the best way to
avoid the predictable is first to state it in one's own preparation
and then subject it to a barrage of questions until it opens up less
predictable avenues for exposition along which the preacher
may proceed. For example, if the subject is salvation, the
predictable thing for an evangelical preacher to say is that a
person is saved from sin through faith in Christ. Now, having
put that down, let the preacher subject it to an onslaught of
questions: What is sin? Is it the same as sinning? If it is
important, why are so many people so unconcerned about it?
Should I tell my non-Christian neighbour that he is a sinner?
What is faith? Is it merely belief? How can someone who lived
2000 years ago save me now? What are we saved *to*? Will the
implications of this subject have a different relevance to
different age-groups within the congregation? The danger of
this approach is that the preacher ends up with far too much
material and may overload his message. But since the purpose
of the exercise is to open up fresh lines of thought, he should
select those that have proved most profitable, expand them, and
reject the rest. For instance, the question about telling one's
neighbour that he is a sinner could well lead to a profitable
sermon section on sharing with the respectable and happy non-
Christian this basic assumption of the gospel.

We can avoid dullness, too by speaking with warmth and
conviction. If a congregation gets the impression that the
preacher is not very excited about the things he is preaching,

they are not going to get excited about them either. It is important for the preacher to look at the people he is speaking to. I have sometimes been in the pew when the preacher has addressed his entire discourse (or I should say, those parts of it when he was not staring at his manuscript) to a point just below the ceiling level at the back wall of the church. I have even found myself turning round to see who this privileged person might be that he should receive such constant attention! This lack of contact and rapport between preacher and congregation creates a detached, remote, almost unreal feeling, as if the preaching isn't really intended for those present and the preacher is hardly aware of their presence.

The use of illustrations also helps to maintain interest. Those drawn from real life experience are best. But care must be taken to ensure that illustrations really do illustrate and are not included to raise a laugh – or even perhaps because of some deep need within the preacher to draw attention to himself. It is perhaps a good idea to try to find one good illustration for each major point. An appropriate real-life illustration is helpful in three ways: it throws light upon the point being made; it helps the hearer to relate the point to his own life; and it gives the mind of the hearer a rest before going on with the discourse.

Dullness is therefore to be avoided, but not at any price. Being funny for the sake of being funny is dishonouring to the gospel. So is being 'clever'. So is the gimmick used for its own sake. Though preaching may be 'truth through personality' – and God can use a colourful personality greatly to his glory – anything which draws attention to the preacher rather than to the preaching, or to the Lord, should be examined very critically before it is allowed to pass.

6. Applying the Message

Many otherwise good sermons fail to be effective because the preachers do not show their congregations how the message can be applied in their lives. One of the most serious communication failures in the church today is that preachers go on telling people what to do and be without telling them how to do and be it. At the risk of appearing to be false to a basic biblical principle, I venture to suggest that our congregations hear far too much about faith and far too little about works. I am not referring to the works of practical and social concern in which the church generally has been much more involved in recent years, but about what might be called the 'works of faith'. The New Testament calls them 'signs and wonders' (Acts 2.43 etc.). Those inside the church and those outside it need to witness people being saved – that is, being made whole; they need to see them being forgiven and healed, growing in maturity and grace, receiving and exercising the gifts of Christ and the Spirit, becoming leaders, preachers, teachers, prophets, pastors, healers. These signs and wonders attracted unbelievers to the church in New Testament days, and their absence from the contemporary church may well be one of the factors contributing to the lack of interest shown by the average unbeliever in the church today.

The objection might be raised that these 'works of faith' are really the result of the gift of the Spirit and therefore not 'works' at all. That is so. But the Spirit's power does not operate in the believer automatically. If it did, Jesus would not have urged his hearers to ask for this power (Luke 11.9–13), nor told them to persist in prayer until their requests were granted (Luke 11.5–8; 18.1–5). The power of the Holy Spirit operates within certain conditions and it is the duty of the preacher to discover those conditions for himself and to tell his hearers what they are. As preachers, we fail our congregations if we refer to the wonderful gifts and resources of God in Christ through the Spirit, without telling them how they may receive these resources and exercise these gifts. To do this – that is, to refer to the resources of God without showing people how to receive them, not only weakens and restricts the ministry and witness of the church, it also increases the Christian's sense of helplessness and frustration. He may leave a service with the conviction that the fullness of the Christian experience is something beyond the range of the ordinary believer. Something for the spiritual elite only.

I try to remember at the end of sermon preparation to ask myself two questions. Firstly, 'So what?' That is the question that brings the subject down the first step from being something purely academic or hypothetical. God loves you. So what? So what difference is that going to make to your life? So what are you going to do about it? The second question is 'And how?'

The answer to that question completes the process of relating the subject specifically to the needs and opportunities of the hearer. God loves me. So what? So I must respond to his love. and how? It is the answer to that question which will determine the effectiveness of the sermon in terms of the production of those 'works of faith' we were considering above.

Preaching as a Shared Ministry

The decline in the popularity of the sermon has been noted above. Whether or not it will ever regain its popularity is a matter for conjecture. What we shall examine now are some suggestions for giving the sermon a place of value and significance in the service of worship, without restoring to it the ethos of the virtuoso performance which it once had. This, I suggest, may be done by treating the sermon as part and product of a shared ministry. By this I do not mean putting more than one person in the pulpit in any given service – though it could include that. I mean the development of a ministry of preaching which is related by conversation, debate and dialogue to the on-going strategy and immediate needs of the church and its people as and where they are.

A good sermon feeds, but the body of Christ must not only be fed. That way it may turn to fat, putting on flesh without developing muscle. And we have seen that happen so often. A healthy body must be fed *with an appropriate diet*. Just as some physical bodies need to avoid fats, others to have more calcium, some to avoid sugar, others to have more vitamins, so the body of Christ as the local church has certain special needs at certain times. The preacher must be able to feed these needs with the appropriate food. (Not forgetting that there are certain basic needs which must be fed all the time.) In order to do this, the preacher must know what the specific needs are. Diagnosis must precede prescription. This means that before he is a speaker, the preacher must be a listener. He must listen, as it were, with one ear to what the people of the church are saying, and with the other ear to what God is saying to the people of the church. The more sensitive the listener, the more effective the speaker.

There is a two-fold difficulty here. One difficulty is that of being sure of what God is saying. This is a matter for the preacher's own walk with God and cannot be considered here. Happy is that congregation whose preacher has come from what used to be called 'the divine audience chamber' and can declare from the pulpit with humble confidence the counsel of God, both whole and specific; who can say with the Old Testament prophet, 'Thus says the Lord', and with the New Testament visionary, 'Hear what the Spirit says to the churches'. The other difficulty is that of discovering what the people are saying. This is particularly difficult because the chances are that they are not saying anything! So many of our people are inarticulate when it comes to spiritual and theological matters. One only has to listen to the vestibule conversation of the average congregation after a service – a time when one might expect religious things to be in the forefront of people's minds – to realize this.

Every opportunity should be sought which will allow sermon-givers to talk to sermon-hearers about sermons. This can be done at different levels. In the Methodist circuit in which I now minister the Local Preachers' Meeting meets occasionally with one of the church councils of the circuit for a frank evaluation of the preaching ministry being offered to that church, and to learn about its specific needs, individual and corporate. The whole question of relevant preaching can be raised in church councils, church meetings, fellowship meetings and house groups, and the 'findings' shared with the circuit preachers. More helpful verbal contact could be made between individuals and preachers. The well-meant 'thank you for your service' muttered over the departing handshake is mildly encouraging, but it does not help very much. Is the person merely being polite? Which part of the service am I being thanked for? Did I say something particularly helpful, and if so, what? If only there could be in every church a lively exchange of views and needs between an honest and seeking congregation and humble and adaptable preachers, the effectiveness of the preaching could be greatly increased.

It is sometimes said that preachers get the congregations they deserve. To a certain extent, the reverse of this is also true: congregations get the preachers they deserve. If congregations show no more interest in the preaching than a polite 'thank you for your service' with the exit handshake, they cannot expect the preaching to be very relevant or helpful.

It was partly to solve this problem of communication between preacher and congregation that an experiment in 'shared preaching' was made in the Chapel Street Methodist Church, Penzance. It began when the parents of some of the senior Sunday school scholars admitted that they did not come regularly to church because they found the worship dull and irrelevant. Sunday services appeared to them to be weekly recitals in words and music prepared and presented by the preacher and organist-choirmaster, without consultation with anyone else (or between themselves for that matter), and with little opportunity for the congregation to be involved either in the conduct of the service itself, or at the ideas and planning stage. They were challenged with the question, 'If a way could be found of giving you an opportunity of sharing in the planning and conduct of services, would you come to them every week?' They said they would. So the six parents involved became the nucleus of a regularly meeting house-group, and set to work to plan services – gaining resources from Bible-study, discussion and prayer. Eight o'clock on Sunday evenings was chosen as the time for the weekly worship because it was a time generally convenient to the group, and a time at which the minister could be free to be present every week.

The venture has proved successful. Starting with one group of eight people, there are now, eighteen months later, seven groups and a growing eight o'clock congregation at present averaging ninety, half of whom were not in regular worship at the church when the venture began. The groups take it in turn to plan and take part in the services. Participation can include reading, prayers, drama, mime, singing and the various acts of stewarding. The actual preaching is normally done by the minister, assisted from time to time by local preachers who attend the service. Subjects for the sermons are suggested by the groups, publicized well in advance and discussed in the groups. The result is that the preacher standing before the eight o'clock congregation has the advantage of knowing that he is about to speak about a subject which the people before him have asked for, upon which their thoughts have already been stimulated, and after which there will be some useful feed-back, either over the refreshments that always follow the services, in a subsequent group meeting, or during pastoral visitation.

In the context of this type of shared preaching, the sermon is no longer a sort of hit-and-miss twenty minute slot which may or may not be relevant and helpful to the hearers, but is part of an integrated, on-going process. A process which begins with a time of listening, is developed through dialogue, consultation and shared prayer, reaches a point of public expression within the worship service, and then continues to live on in the response of the hearers and in further discussion and application. Furthermore, the preacher who is aware of the actual condition of his congregation, and of the word of the Lord to that condition, will be endued with a quality often absent from preaching today – expectancy. Knowing that he is truly bringing together the actual needs and aspirations of the people and the resources of God, the preacher will look for results, and he will see them. He is privileged to stand in the crucial and exciting place between those things which have been given and done – the promises of God and the finished work of Christ applicable through the Holy Spirit; and the things that are to be and are to be done – the fulfilment of those promises and the fruit of Christ's work.

Notes

1. *Beyond the Churches*, MARC 1984.
2. *The Methodist Service Book*, The Methodist Publishing House 1975, pp. A7, A21.

6

CHRISTIAN EDUCATION
David G. Sharp

Whatever we call the subject of this chapter – and any one of the usual designations has its drawbacks – it is vital to the ministry of the church. 'Education' may conjure up in people's minds visions of rows of desks. 'Training' suggests either physical jerks or preparation for specific tasks. 'All-age Sunday school' sounds too juvenile. But while we may need to find a more appropriate title, one that will not put people off, there is one truth that we cannot escape. All those who have responded to Christ's call to be disciples have responded to a call to learn, for the Greek word for disciple, *mathētēs*, actually means 'learner'. The church therefore is committed to the teaching and learning business.

I have been in the teaching and learning business for most of my life, on one side of the desk or the other. That experience has led me to the conclusion that there are no simple blueprints for Christian education. What this chapter hopes to do, therefore, is to raise questions, rather than provide detailed answers. I am particularly indebted to two authors, whose books are recommended for careful study: Jennifer Rogers, *Adults Learning*[1] and Gordon Jones, *Design for Learning*.[2]

This chapter will be dealing with general principles of Christian education. For simplicity's sake, therefore, most of the examples and applications refer to the education of adults in our churches. However, it should not be difficult to apply what is said here to our teaching of children. Moreover, there is a wealth of material available in the field of children's Christian education for those who wish to pursue that aspect of the church's task.

Aims

A weakness of Christian thinking on education is to confuse general aims with specific objectives. We need both to know in a general sense where we are going, and the detailed stages by which we hope to get there. This section seeks to suggest general directions. It is not exhaustive, but offers two contrasting formulations of aims in Christian education for discussion.

(a) Gordon Jones, based on Ephesians 4.12:

1. The training and mobilizing of a live nucleus within the congregation. This would form the spiritual heart of the church with whom the minister can openly share his hopes and prayers. Here the elders will be discovered and trained to become themselves teachers of others.
2. The training and mobilizing of the congregation as a whole. Neglecting no area of need, anxious always to discover new potential and new gifts to engage in the work plan. The whole church needs to understand the principles upon which continuous mission becomes a reality.
3. The training and work of servicing the parish's continuous mission, both locally and beyond.[3]

(b) David Sheppard, Bishop of Liverpool:

I hope that education will offer children . . . : equipment with basic tools to go on learning; a vision of greatness, leading to ideals of personal and corporate behaviour; awareness of the whole community and the wider world; confidence in the gifts they possess and ambition to use them for the good of the community; respect for reasoned authority; creative discontent with society as it is and experience of bringing about changes for good.[4]

With these two definitions in mind, it may be helpful to attempt a formulation of our own. What is the ultimate objective of Christian learning? Here are some biblical statements: 'The way to become wise is to honour the Lord' (Ps. 111.10); 'None of them will have to teach his fellow-countryman to know the Lord, because all will know me' (Jer. 31.34); 'Take my yoke and put it on you, and learn from me' (Matt.

11.29); 'All I want is to know Christ' (Phil. 3.10). Verses such as these suggest that our goal in Christian education is not so much theoretical or doctrinal knowledge, but a personal relationship with God, a knowledge of and obedience to him.

Or again, how far should a Christian education programme provide us with answers and how far cause us to ask the right questions? God in the Bible often enters into discussion with his people; through the prophets, e.g. 'Now let's settle the matter . . . ' (Isa. 1.18); through Jesus, e.g. in the Sermon on the Mount 'Isn't life worth more than food? Can any of you live a bit longer by worrying about it?' (Matt. 6.25, 27). The Bereans were led by Paul's preaching to 'criticize' or 'ask questions of' the scriptures (Acts 17.11). A book like Ronald Sider's *Rich Christians in an Age of Hunger*[5] raises questions in our minds about Christian life-styles. One could argue on such grounds that the goal of Christian education is to instil a way of thinking rather than (or at least, as well as) a body of thought.

When we are thinking about our goal, we should not forget the passages describing Jesus' confrontation with the religious authorities (e.g. Mark 7.1–23). He condemned them for, in effect, making a god out of the system that they taught. We must avoid falling into the same trap – which we may do if we place too much emphasis on the *imparting of a body of Christian truth* as the goal of Christian education. That suggests that, once we have assimilated a particular 'text-book', we have arrived. But the Christian disciple, by definition, never takes off his 'L-plates'. Our Christian education programme should lead us all to share the attitude of St Paul: 'I keep striving . . . I do my best to reach what is ahead. I run straight towards the goal . . . ' (Phil. 3.10–16).

Objectives

Once we know where we are going, we can begin to plan the route. This will involve asking basic questions, which we often neglect to do. It is simpler to adopt a ready-made programme of church training and assume it will fit our situation. A little thought, however, will help us to avoid the disappointment which sometimes arises over such 'package deals'.

For example: Whom are we teaching (their educational

background, ability to cope with the proposed programme, anxieties and expectations about it, maturity)? Our first task is to know our potential learners, which will take time and, perhaps, some form of survey or questionnaire. Who is to do the teaching (experience, ability to cope with the proposed material and methods)? Is it to be the minister, or is he prepared to acknowledge that there are those with a teaching gift in the congregation? What do we want to be able to see that we have achieved at the end of the programme? It is essential that the learners should know that they have learned something when it is all over! Some courses set such far-away goals that the poor learners are totally discouraged from the beginning. Achieving long-term aims seems much more possible when they are broken down into specific short-term objectives. Consider Jesus' remark to his disciples (John 16.12): 'I have much more to tell you, but now it would be too much for you to bear.'

Finally, having clear objectives helps the education process in at least four ways:

(a) teaching and learner both know what they are doing;
(b) the teacher is enabled to structure his course clearly;
(c) he is able to decide on appropriate teaching activities;
(d) it is easy to check the learner's progress.

The Programme

There are many packaged Christian learning programmes available, but as we think about our objectives, we may come to the conclusion that none really fits our situation. How then should we set about drawing up our own programme?

Most teaching in most churches is attempted from the pulpit, and this means in fact that the programme is imposed by the preacher on the congregation. This happens, first, because there is usually little feed-back from the congregation, and, secondly, because many preachers resent being tied to a lectionary or asked to preach on a specific topic. This is said to limit the freedom of the Holy Spirit: but does he work only in preachers and not in congregations or lectionary compilers?

Consider Jesus' teaching: much of it arose in response to questions (e.g. Mark 7.1–20) or to deal with situations the disciples met (e.g. Mark 9.28–29, 38–50). The same is frequently true of Paul's letters (e.g. I Corinthians, in which he deals with a string of matters the Corinthians have asked about in their letter to him). How often do we gear our teaching to the questions our people are really asking? How much truth is there in the comments that the preacher is ten feet above contradiction, answering questions that no-one is asking?

At a conference on theological education Derek Rowntree of the Open University summed up the curriculum or programme as a 'negotiated compromise between:

(a) the requirements of the system;
(b) the capabilities of the teacher;
(c) what the learners want to learn'.

What is true in the college situation is also true in the church. There is a body of belief to be communicated ('the system'), but not all ministers or leaders will be equipped to teach all of it, and some of it may not be relevant to a particular congregation at a particular time.

The present writer tries to practise this principle of negotiated compromise in, for example, church membership classes. A questionnaire given to all participants at the beginning asks them to indicate any particular problems or topics they would like to discuss during the course. These are then dovetailed at appropriate points into the basic teaching on Christian discipleship and church membership which has to be covered. And for certain topics, other leaders are brought in so that the group may benefit from their experience in their own field, e.g. a physics teacher to talk about science and faith.

We need to work out how we can apply this principle to all teaching/learning situations in the church, so that the learners feel that they have a stake in the programme. The minister should not expect to be the only person who knows what is good for the congregation.

The Teacher

Teaching is a communication process: something takes place between teacher and learner, between person and person. There ought certainly to be transmission of information, but that does not happen in a vacuum. Because persons are involved, personality plays an important part in the teaching process.

The writer can still recall the problems he had over the place of personality in preaching in his early days as a preacher. A preacher's personality, he had been told, should not intrude between the word of God and the hearers. It took a long time for the realization to dawn that God communicate via the personality of the preacher – or there is no real communication at all.

What is true of preaching is true of teaching, whatever method is employed. Thus when Jennifer Rogers paints the portrait of the ideal teacher, the features which stand out are to a large degree traits of personality. Her list is as follows:

(a) a warm personality, which expresses approval and acceptance of those being taught;
(b) social skill, to weld the group of learners together;
(c) an indirect manner of teaching, which will make use of the students' ideas;
(d) conscientious efficiency;
(e) skill in identifying and resolving difficulties – which requires not just mastery of the subject taught but understanding of the people learning, or trying to learn;
(f) enthusiasm, which will show itself, for example, in eye-contact with the learning group and variety in the use of the voice.

'Adult teachers lose no status and create no problems for themselves by enjoying the friendship of their classes, nor need they feel they have to act a part, conceal their ignorance and display only their strengths.' In other words, a teacher in a Christian education programme should be himself and allow God to use him.

Consider the impact made by Jesus as a teacher. It was not only what he said, but how he said it: e.g. Matt. 7.28–29, 'When Jesus finished saying these things, the crowd was amazed at the way he taught. He wasn't like the teachers of the Law; instead, he taught with authority.' Notice, too, how he practised the skills of a good teacher, welding together as his pupils a most unlikely group of individuals (e.g. Mark 3.13–19), taking up the ideas and questions in his listeners' minds (e.g. Mark 3.22ff.), never afraid to look his hearers in the eye and offer them love and acceptance (e.g. Mark 3.33–35).

Those of us who believe we have been called to teach have also been commissioned to find other teachers (cf. II Tim. 2.2). What qualities do we look for? Do we make young people teachers just to keep them in the Sunday school? Do we assume that preachers will also be teachers? It may be difficult for a preacher to adapt his style when out of the pulpit: he may dominate his group of learners – and then there is the danger that the group will become dependent on him as a kind of 'guru'. (Do we see evidence of this happening with the development of tape ministries?) If the church is to fulfil its teaching/learning role, then we must seek out, recognize and use to the full those teaching gifts that God has distributed among the church's members.

The Learners

It seems today that, wherever one turns in a discussion of learning, one meets, sooner or later, this old Chinese proverb:

I hear and I forget;
I see and I remember;
I do and I understand.

It points us immediately to one of the essentials, which is, paradoxically, also one of the difficulties, of the learning process: participation.

Children are unselfconscious about participation, whether it is reciting tables, repeating language drills, or doing the actions to choruses. The transition to secondary school, however, seems to mark a point at which such childish things are put away, and by the time adulthood is reached participation is harder to achieve. Indeed, as Jennifer Rogers points out, many adult students tend to be nervous about any learning in which they are expected to participate actively (language classes, discussion groups, cookery).

What is true of secular adult education is true in the church also. Some people even feel threatened if they think they might be asked to read a lesson in church. And yet the most efficient learning takes place when there is strong motivation (with nervousness therefore at a minimum) and plenty of active participation. We shall return to this under *Methods* (see below).

But what about the learning capacity of the people in our churches? Another proverb says that you cannot teach an old dog new tricks. That is not strictly true: it is possible, but it may be more difficult. For example, the older we get, the less efficient our short-term memory becomes. Who has not known a grandparent, or other elderly person, who could recite poetry learned in youth but not remember what happened last week? Vision and hearing are both at their best when we are in our teens. (All preachers are familiar with the old ladies who sit at the back and complain they cannot hear or read the hymn numbers!) And yet, if the slowing down of faculties with age is taken into account, adults will learn just as efficiently as young people.

Whether or not we participate and learn is largely a matter of expectation. If we expect that the minister (or other church leader) is there to run the church and do everything, and our only responsibility is to attend a service once a week and put money in the plate to keep the system going, we will do nothing and learn nothing. Unfortunately there have been church leaders who have treated people as if that was all that *was* expected of them. If, however, we have grasped that being a Christian and a church member is an activity, a process of learning and growing and of involvement, and we expect something to happen, the result will be entirely different. We must therefore seek to cultivate and encourage the attitude of the Bereans (Acts 17.11) who were eager to learn, and open-minded and ready to ask the right kind of questions.

We must also ask ourselves some questions: How do I see being a church member? What do I expect of my minister? What does he seem to expect of me? If we are ministers or leaders: What do I expect of my congregation? Do I encourage and facilitate their participation, or do I like to keep my authoritarian position? Hard questions, but ones which must be asked if the education process is to go forward.

Methods

In a short survey like this it will be impossible to do more than indicate general principles, and refer briefly to some of the many methods available to the teacher today. For a full discussion of the different methods the reader should consult Rogers, or the similar (though less full) study, *Teaching Techniques in Adult Education*.[6]

1. The Setting For Learning

What has already been said about the nervousness of many adults as they approach learning, especially learning in which participation is expected of them, makes the first condition for learning obvious: the atmosphere must be relaxing. So what sort of room should we meet in? How are the chairs arranged? (It is amazing what a difference putting the chairs in a circle makes even to a church business meeting. There can be no more chuntering on the back row while the meeting goes on in front. Everybody is in the group.) Are they comfortable? Can everyone hear and see? Some people look for any excuse to switch off! Consider how Jesus drew the disciples aside away from the pressures of the crowds to teach them as a small group (e.g. Mark 6.30–32).

This leads on to the question of numbers. How many can we teach effectively at once? The educationalists tell us that if we wish to have the active participation of group members, then eight to twelve is the optimum size. (How many disciples did Jesus call and teach as the nucleus of the new people of God?) Bishop John V. Taylor[7] has some interesting comments on the possibilities of re-structuring the church for growth (which includes learning) around small cell groups. He concludes: 'It is the "little congregations" which must become normative if the church is to respond to the Spirit's movements in the life of the world.' In Methodism the division of the society into classes, each under a leader, used to provide this structure. Do we have its equivalent today? Do we need it?

It follows, of course, that in the small group, as opposed to the large congregation/lecture audience, every member can be known individually by the teacher and by other members of the group. He or she can be addressed personally (and it is vital that the teacher learns everyone's name), feel acceptance by the rest of the group and therefore be willing to contribute.[8]

It follows also that the teacher's style must be such as to put people at ease. A good teacher will be like a good host. There will be a proper place for laughter as a tension-relaxer, for people will not want to continue coming if they feel under stress. After all, why should one not enjoy Christian education? And what about those preachers who always begin with an amusing anecdote rather than the solemn announcement of a text? Some of Jesus' parables are fairly outrageous, when you think about it (e.g. Matt. 7.1–5). The trouble is that we have heard them so often that we no longer see the humour in them. But we do not consider them as inappropriate aids to teaching.

Finally, under this general heading: no session should end, even the first and most introductory, without the group being able to say 'we have learned something.' Better still, in the context of Christian education, they should be able to echo the words of the disciples on the road to Emmaus (Luke 24.32): 'Wasn't it like a fire burning in us when he talked to us on the road and explained the scriptures to us?' For, in the last analysis, in Christian education we are all, teachers and learners, on the road with the great teacher, and it should show. 'The members of the Council were amazed to see how bold Peter and John were and to learn that they were ordinary men of no education. They realized then that they had been companions of Jesus' (Acts 4.13). There may perhaps be more than a grain of truth in the old saying: Christianity is caught, not taught.

2. *Specific Teaching Methods*

'Too much faith is commonly placed in oral lessons and lectures. To be poured into like a bucket is not exhilarating to any soul' (Thomas Carlyle, quoted by Jennifer Rogers). The lecture or oral lesson is probably the method with which most of us are most familiar, especially those with any professional training. And we all preach, or listen to, sermons every week. So when we think of teaching, we automatically think of this method first. Yet it has proven failings, especially with adults. For example, it places a strain on weak short-term memories. Feedback is difficult, unless the lecturer is prepared to stop frequently. It demands of the learners the ability to take notes. On the other hand, it can be used effectively to convey information. When it *is* used, it should be kept short and have a clearly defined structure (like a good sermon) so that the listeners can follow easily the train of thought and pick out the

essential information that is being imparted. The lecture
method becomes even more effective when used in conjunction
with other methods, or with written materials (worksheets,
charts, diagrams), so that the learner is transformed from being
a passive listener into an active participant in the learning
process.

In church situations there is room for experiment here. We
are accustomed to our Sunday school children having 'take-
home leaflets' which reinforce the class teaching by giving the
children things to do afterwards. How about a 'take-home
leaflet' for the congregation, based on the sermon? Or the use of
an overhead projector or other aid (chart, slides) to provide a
visual element in the teaching process? For while Sunday
worship and preaching are not primarily intended as a teaching
medium, with many of our people they are our only opportunity for teaching, and we must therefore make the most effective
use of them. But let us not be 'gimmicky' for the sake of it: 'Is
there not something more than linguistically incongruous about
the blind leading the blind by means of visual aids?'[9] We will
perhaps learn how to use visual aids from a re-reading of our
Bibles, noting how God has used them to communicate with us
(e.g. Jeremiah's visit to the potter's house, Jer. 18.1–12; or
Jesus' use of scenes from every-day life in his parables).

But if we are seeking optimum learning conditions, that is
active participation by our learners in small, co-operative
groups, then we shall want to use other methods too. We are
familiar with the idea of discussion groups. They also can have
their drawbacks. They can become just a lecture under another
name if the leader makes them a platform for his own opinions.
The chapters in Rogers's and Jones's books note some of the
pitfalls and provide advice, and there are many other aids to
discussion available, e.g.: *Your Turn to Lead*,[10] specifically on
Bible discussion groups or the discussion book by J. Hills
Cotterill.[11]

While in discussion members of a group may remain
relatively detached, there is one series of teaching methods that
leads to full involvement, and which therefore should perhaps
not be attempted until the teacher has the group's full
confidence. These are the methods dealt with by Rogers in her
chapter: *Case Study, Role-Play, Simulation Games*. Briefly, in

these methods teacher and learners imagine themselves into situations (which become increasingly realistic as one moves through the series), and learn by working out how to deal with them. They have in common the fact that they are all based on real life situations; all require participation by the learner; in all of them the learner not only has to acquire knowledge but to use it, and to use knowledge correctly demands understanding. It does not require great imagination to see that there are many instances in our church life where such methods would be most appropriate (e.g. training Sunday school teachers, pastoral visitors or church stewards).

This would apply even to the teaching of Christian doctrine because Christianity as revealed in the Bible is not a series of abstract religious ideas. The doctrines of Christianity arise out of situations in which God acted in certain ways (e.g. the doctrine of grace from the way in which God acts towards people and individuals without regard to their merit, choosing Israel, offering the gospel to both Jews and Gentiles, etc.). And Christian doctrine is not revealed for its own sake but to prompt us to Christian action in specific situations (e.g. as God has been gracious to us we are to be gracious and forgiving towards others). With a little imagination, therefore, we can reinforce even the teaching of doctrine by methods involving role-play or other forms of active participation.

Maryk in Herman Wouk's *The Caine Mutiny* tells how he passed his naval exams by repeating word for word one page of the gunnery manual which neither he nor any of his fellow examinees could understand. That is not education, it is a feat of memory, and it is not very difficult to reproduce similar feats. In our Christian education programmes, however, we must use methods which will lead not just to knowledge about Christianity, but to that understanding of God which produces transformed lives.

From 'Peanuts' by Schulz.

Sally: How come you won't help me with my home work?

Charlie Brown: You don't really want help . . . What you really want is someone else to do the work for you!

Sally: THAT'S EDUCATION, ISN'T IT?!

Notes

1. Jennifer Rogers, *Adults Learning*, Open University 1977 (second edition).

2. Gordon Jones, *Design for Learning*, Falcon Books 1974.

3. Jones, op. cit., p. 84.

4. David Sheppard, *Built as a City*, Hodder and Stoughton 1974, p. 133.

5. Ronald Sider, *Rich Christians in an Age of Hunger*, Hodder and Stoughton 1978.

6. M. S. Stephens and G. W. Roderick (eds), *Teaching Techniques in Adult Education*, David and Charles 1971.

7. John V. Taylor, *The Go-Between God*, SCM Press 1972, pp. 146ff.

8. There is a useful chapter on how groups work in *Design for Learning*, which is the basis of a soundstrip available from Falcon Visual Aids, 32 Fleet Street, London EC4Y 1DB.

9. A. P. F. Sell on Preaching, *Evangelical Quarterly*, April-June 1974.

10. Margaret Parker, *Your Turn to Lead*, Scripture Union 1973.

11. J. Hills Cotterill, *Let's Talk it Through*, Key Books, Scripture Union 1975.

7

CHURCH MEMBERSHIP

Howard Mellor

New Testament Teaching

In the New Testament we find the early Christians struggling to understand the nature of the church of which they had become a part If we are to build up a picture of what church membership means today then we do well to start by considering its meaning and implication for them.

The Acts of the Apostles and the New Testament epistles not only tell the story of how the church grew, they relate the missionary methods and show the influences that undermined their work, as well as their joys and victories in sharing the good news.

Keeping track of the growing membership of the emerging church was no simple matter, as new believers were added daily to the community of Christians (Acts 2.41, 47). Whilst it would seem unlikely that they had a pastoral committee, they certainly knew who was a part of the Christian community, to the extent that they could remove a person from membership after a discipline case (I Cor. 5.2).

The church is a fellowship of believers who have responded to the proclaimed word of God and who believe in Jesus Christ and confess him as Lord (Rom. 10.9). It is personal faith in Jesus Christ that brings the church into being, for the church consists of those who call on the name of the Lord Jesus Christ (I Cor. 1.2). By definition it is being a follower of Christ that makes any of us a Christian, but clearly to be numbered among the fellowship of Christians is important. The process of caring for one another, learning together, breaking bread and praising God are essential features in the Christian's life (Acts 2.44–47).

The church is a universal community of faith. This corporate nature of church membership is highlighted by some of the titles given to Christians in the New Testament. They are the *ekklēsia* and the body of Christ.[1] They are the people of God. They are part of the kingdom of God, for they are a fellowship of men and women under his rule.

Why Become a Church Member?

There are in every church a number of people who worship regularly and yet seem not to feel the need to become full members of the church. Below we note some of the points most frequently discussed when the question of membership is posed.

1. 'I'm Not Good Enough'

We need to say quite clearly that none of us is good enough, but, thank God, there is hope for us all. It is precisely the recognition that we are not good enough that points us towards Jesus, his church and our part in it. If it were necessary for us to qualify by being 'good' then none would be church members or receive communion. Nor would there be any preachers.

It is encouraging to notice the people Jesus chose to be his disciples. Far from being 'good' they were sometimes arrogant and argumentative. They deserted Jesus and yet at the same time were eager to learn and follow him. Jesus did not seek out 'good' people, but rather, by his teaching and example, he helped to mould those he called to be his disciples.

2. 'I Don't Agree with all the Church Does and Says'

Because we are made unique by a creator God it would be surprising if we did all agree. The Acts of the Apostles shows how people of different cultural backgrounds and different expectations have disagreements and yet learn to live together and to love one another.

For myself I am as much a member of my particular denomination for the things with which I disagree (involving myself in discussion of these issues) as I am committed to it because of the things in our doctrine and practice that I rejoice over. Some evangelicals have turned away from main-line denominations because of this very point. We would urge them to stay and involve themselves as full members of their church in its life and witness. The church will not become what we feel, under God, it could be unless we are committed to it and working in it. And of course there is always the sobering thought that we might not always be right, and the church might not always be wrong in its theology and practice.

3. 'The People are not My Type'

We may be hesitant and unsure whether we shall fit in and be accepted by the regular members of the church. Perhaps our hesitation is because we are young and they are all elderly; we are professional people and they will not understand the pressures we are under; we wonder whether they will really want a one-parent family; we are quiet and they all seem so confident; they all seem to have been here for ages, and they all know one another and many of them seem to be inter-related. God protect us from monochrome churches! We are all one in Christ, and a mixture of age, background, ability and temperament brings a richness to the worship and fellowship of our church. Where better to proclaim that unity than in a local church? The promise of acceptance and belonging is what gives substance to our talk of fellowship.

The answers to the question 'Why become a church member?' are not all negative, however. There are some clear and positive reasons, and we look at these now.

1. Declaration of Faith

Public reception into full membership or confirmation gives the opportunity for each person to make an open confession of faith to the congregation. This is one of the reasons why it is desirable that reception into full membership should be a part of the main service of the day. We discuss later ways in which this declaration of faith can be incorporated into the service itself.

2. Commitment to other Christians

We have seen that the New Testament images of the church

are corporate, indicating an interdependence of individual Christians. Membership is a sign of our commitment to those with whom we worship and whom we have grown to love. It is a sign of our trust and our desire to grow and mature together as a Christian people. We make it clear that ours is not a take-it-or-leave-it attitude to what the church can offer; our presence does not depend on mood or inclination. Rather membership becomes a sign of our commitment to work out and make real the injunction of Jesus that we should love one another as he has loved us (John 15.12).

3. Wider Opportunity for Service

As a full member of the church we can give greater service to and through the church. We may be invited to serve on various committees or take up one of the offices in the church. We may be able to serve the community on behalf of and in the name of the church. The scope for exercising the gifts that God has given us becomes greater, and that kind of ministry together is where Christians grow in grace and maturity as they serve in the name of Christ.

How Do I Become a Member?

The question can be answered administratively as well as pastorally. The detailed procedure varies from one denomination to another. In the Church of England the incumbent is responsible for the decision as to which candidates shall be presented to the Bishop as ready for confirmation. In different Free Churches the names of those desiring membership are proposed to the Church Council, the Pastoral Committee, or the deacons or elders.

In all denominations a preparation class or confirmation class is arranged at which, over a period of months, candidates are trained. The aim of these classes is well expressed in my own denomination in the words: 'Members in training shall be instructed in the way of Christian salvation with the aim of securing or deepening in each of them a real, personal and lasting covenant with God in Christ.'[2]

The committee that has pastoral responsibility will want to be assured of each candidate's sincere acceptance of the basis of membership in that church and the evidence of that sincerity in life and conduct, in attendance at worship and in engaging in and maintaining the fellowship. When they are satisfied a public reception or confirmation is arranged for these members.

Standards such as these make it clear that what we are considering is the training and reception of new disciples into the life of the church: it is a far cry from the situation where the only requirement seemed to be that the candidate had reached the age of thirteen.

All denominations call upon their members to serve Christ in the life of the church and in the world. Let us explore in more detail what this means.

1. In the Church

The *Short Guide to Church Membership* issued every year to all Methodists gives a summary of what is involved in serving Christ in the church that would no doubt be agreed by most active Christians in all denominations: 'A member is committed to worship, Holy Communion, fellowship and service, prayer and Bible study, and responsible giving.'

The statement in Acts 2.44–47 that the early Christians were 'together' indicates the quality of their fellowship rather than simply meaning that they were in the same place. Jesus points to this loving fellowship as being a means of evangelism (John 13.35).

The Christian life is a dynamic relationship, not a static designation, and it needs to grow and mature in the context of a sharing, learning, worshipping church. It is the context of *agapē*, of loving Christian interaction that shows itself in support, the exercise of gifts, study and prayer. These things are themselves the springboard of mission and service.

2. In the World

The same *Short Guide* goes on to say: 'A member is committed to the working out of his faith in daily life, the offering of personal service in the community, the Christian use of his resources and the support of the Church in its total world mission.'

Christian truth must be visible before it is audible. A response to Christ is altogether a life-style response. The

Christian life is not restricted to a few hours on Sunday, but it is a total commitment to Christ and his teaching in every part of life: home, family and friends, work and leisure. It is the sort of people we are that will show others our faith (See Gal. 5.22–24).

The creation narrative teaches us that this is God's world and as his people we are stewards of it. Therefore the Christian and the Christian church need to be seen to respond to environmental and community issues, whether globally or locally. Moreover the Christian has a responsibility to strive for an end to violence and injustice, to establish communities of caring and hope where there is distrust and fear, and to create influences of peace and harmony in the whole created order.

Christian faith, however, needs also to be audible as well as visible. If God's grace has come to us in Christ Jesus, then most assuredly he goes with us in our mission and service. And as we strive to care for the local and global community, God by his Holy Spirit creates situations in which we have opportunity to share our faith. Every Christian should be ready to grasp these willingly. Peter put it like this: 'Always be prepared to make a defence to anyone who calls you to account for the hope that is in you' (I Peter 3.15).

The commission to the church is to preach the good news, making disciples of all nations (Matt. 28.18–20; Luke 24.47). Thus the nature of discipleship is that we are all witnesses to the faith. This liberates witnessing from being the prerogative of the preacher to where it is assuredly most effective: in the naming of Christ in our daily lives.

So Christian truth needs to be both visible and audible. It is important to see the Christian witness in this way rather than as an either/or. If people do not see in us the fruits of our belief they will not listen to what we call good news; moreover we have not gained the right to tell it. Likewise unless we tell the Christian faith how will people be able to interpret the action of our lives and service?

The Services for Entry into the Church

1. Baptism
An earlier chapter in this book has dealt with the background

and meaning of the sacrament of baptism.[3] We shall confine ourselves to its liturgical setting.

The service for the baptism of infants can properly be called a family sacrament. Quite obviously the child is involved, but so are the parents, and no less significantly. The promises they make have implications for their whole life-style and connexion with the church. The service for reception into full membership or confirmation is therefore one that confirms the original promises made in faith. The person may now make the professions of faith his or her own. We do an injustice to both infant baptism and confirmation when we see these two services as unconnected.

The number of people becoming full church members who are not already baptized is increasing. There is less social pressure on parents 'to have their children done'. There is also a growing recognition in all churches practising infant baptism that the promises in the baptism service mean a great deal, and some parents decide that they are not able to make them. Others coming forward for membership have not been baptized in infancy because their parents attended a church practising believers' baptism. Indeed some parents in churches that baptize infants now ask instead for a service of dedication, preferring their children to receive baptism as believers.

All the main denominations except the Baptists recognize this diversity of practice. The Church of England has a variety of orders of service in its Alternative Services Book to provide for the baptism of infants and adult believers. The Methodist Church provides a service for the baptism of those who are able to answer for themselves, and this is linked, as in the Church of England, with confirmation.

Among the Free Churches, the United Reformed Church shows the clearest recognition of the diversity of views among its members, and sees a dual practice of infant baptism and confirmation or dedication and believers' baptism and confirmation as contributing postively to the church as a whole.

2. *The Confirmation Service*

When a person has decided to follow Christ and wishes to declare this by becoming a full church member, this should be a time of great rejoicing in the church. The service for public reception into church membership, or confirmation as it is called in many churches, should be made well known to all the church family. At a time when even many church members think of the church as in decline and give in to pessimism we need to keep before them the fact that today people still respond to the good news. Members should not just be observers of an act of testimony, but should be invited to be participants as they renew their own commitment to Christ and the church.

Whereas in the Church of England confirmation is performed by a bishop, in the Free Churches the one who has pastoral charge of the church, normally of course the local minister, is usually the one who publicly receives the new members. However, the church body should certainly be involved in the welcoming process. Members may take parts of the service such as readings, or where appropriate a member may preach the sermon. In some churches a representative member will be involved in extending a welcome on behalf of all the members.

In churches where it is the practice for communicants to kneel at the communion rail to receive the elements at the Lord's Supper, it is usual for the new members to receive communion at the first table. Members of their families often appreciate being invited to receive communion or a blessing with the new members.

One addition I find helpful is to include individual personal testimony at the point in the service at which the new members make their promises and profession of faith. Testimony is extremely powerful, and always puts before members and adherents alike the fact that commitment to Christ is central to church membership. This can be done in a number of ways, depending on local practice and the gifts of those coming into membership. What I have done is to ask a question, before those provided in the order of service, which sparks off their testimony. We spend a great deal of time on this in the membership class, each telling our story of coming to faith in Jesus, and then agreeing a question that brings out the story. Consequently each question, like every testimony, is unique. This gives people a framework, and it means that within that framework we meet the needs of each person, whether capable at speaking or rather diffident.

Training for Full Church Membership

Reference has already been made to the church membership preparation or confirmation class. A few things remain to be said about this.

Because the course may be spread over five or six months there is a great opportunity to develop relationships with and between the members of the group. In this process the group becomes a model of the church and helps people to feel they belong.

For this reason it is not unimportant that the leaders should be skilled in group work. The minister may have this gift, but equally it could be the gift of a lay person, with the minister invited in for certain sessions. I would suggest that it is more important that the group works well than that the minister leads it.

During the membership training it is sometimes useful, especially when people are unfamiliar with our practice, to invite key people from various parts of church life to explain their role. These may include pastoral oversight, church family, outreach programme, support for mission both at home and overseas, neighbourhood care and the financing of the church. In a stewardship church, time, talents and treasure is a useful outline scheme.

Being a Member

Confirmation as we have described it is just the beginning. The reception service is a commissioning to the service of Christ and the church alongside and supported by other Christians. That support will be needed on a continuing basis.

1. Sharing in Groups

Research into today's growing churches confirms that in order to feel supported each member needs the intimate fellowship of a small sharing group, whether it is called a house group, cell, welcome group, nurture group or class meeting. Such groups, if their leaders take their responsibilities seriously, can provide tremendous support and be the source of spiritual help and guidance to the members, who learn together the true meaning of Christian fellowship as they pray, study and open their hearts to one another.

2. Discerning and Deploying the Gifts

As people come into full church membership we should be anxious to ensure that their gifts are recognized and used. The New Testament is clear that each Christian has a gift to be evoked and employed in the life of the church (I Peter 4.10; I Cor. 12.4–11). Our problem is that when there is a new person in membership we immediately see that one as a candidate for the vacancy no one wants to fill. So often by this method we put square pegs into round holes. This is a reversal of New Testament thinking, where first there is the discernment of the gift a person has, followed by the deployment of that gift in the life of the church.

3. Recognizing Individual Needs

Unfortunately every church has some who can be classified as 'submarine' members. They are easily identified. They disappear from view for indefinite periods, occasionally surfacing into worship. This may have a variety of causes. Do they disappear because worship is so predictably dull, coming only occasionally just to see if it is the same as ever? If so, there is no need to return for a while. Perhaps people are prevented from coming by work or family commitments, and, instead of our demands for their presence, they need our support and care. Or of course it may be that absence from the life of the church is an indication of their lack of commitment to Christ, and their wish no longer to be a part of the church.

In other words we need to know our members well, and those with pastoral responsibilities within the church are the key people. They should be aware of the needs of and the demands on the people in their pastoral care. Only in this way can proper support be given.

The pastoral leaders of a church need to meet together with others to consider every aspect of the care of the members. It is part of their task both to encourage them and also to discipline them. They must ensure that a real attempt is made to encourage absentees to come back into the life of the church and to renew their commitment to Christ and his teaching. We should pray and work that this attempt may succeed.

Growing in the Faith

In his parables Jesus often used models of growth and development such as the grain of mustard, vines, seed, to describe the Christian message and the Christian life. It is not surprising therefore that other writers in the New Testament continue this theme, seeing the Christian faith and our living in it as a dynamic process in which God's spirit is at work in us.

This growth comes in the context of the worship and fellowship of the church. Its soil is found in our prayers and Bible reading, in the encouragement of sharing and learning with other Christians and in the service offered in the name of Christ in the church and local community.

Paul's prayer for the Ephesian Christians is our prayer for all members of our church:[4]

> For this reason I bow my knees before the Father, from whom every family in heaven and on earth is named, that according to the riches of his glory he may grant you to be strengthened with might through his Spirit in the inner man, and that Christ may dwell in your hearts through faith; that you, being rooted and grounded in love, may have power to comprehend with all the saints what is the breadth and length and height and depth, and to know the love of Christ which surpasses knowledge, that you may be filled with all the fulness of God.
>
> Now to him who by the power at work within us is able to do far more abundantly than all we ask or think, to him be glory in the church and in Christ Jesus to all generations, for ever and ever. Amen.

Notes

1. See chapter 1, 'The Local Church'.
2. *The Constitutional Practice and Discipline of the Methodist Church*, Standing Orders 801–804.
3. See chapter 3, 'The Sacraments'.
4. Eph. 3.14–21.

8

CHRISTIAN UNITY

John Job

The vote of rejection for the proposed covenant in the synod of the Church of England at its meeting in July 1982 may well prove to be the end of an epoch. Just where to place the beginning of that epoch may be a matter for discussion. But a convenient point from which to start in any attempt to put the present ecumenical picture into historical perspective is the Lambeth Conference of 1888.

This was the moment when four points were agreed upon, forming what has been called the Lambeth Quadrilateral, and constituting a minimum basis of agreement for reunion with other churches. The doctrinal elements concerned were (a) the Bible; (b) the Apostles' and Nicene Creeds; (c) the two dominical sacraments; and (d) the historic episcopate.

The Question of Episcopacy

None of the first three of these points has ever been an issue in subsequent negotiations. It is the fourth which has always been the focus of controversy.

What then is the historic episcopate? In 1930 the Lambeth Conference defined the term. The argument ran that by the end of the second century AD episcopacy had no effective rivals, and that in this historical development it occupied a position analogous to that of the canon of scripture and the creeds.

What we uphold is the episcopate, maintained in successive generations by continuity of succession and consecration, as it has been throughout the history of the church from the earliest times, and discharging those functions which from the earliest time it has discharged . . . Our special responsibility as an episcopal church is to bring into the complete life of the united church those elements which we have received and hold in trust. Chief among these, in the matter of order, is the historic episcopate.

In the light of this declaration it is easy to see why in his famous sermon in Cambridge in 1946, which was the immediate prelude to conversations between the Church of England and the Methodist Church, Archbishop Fisher invited the Free Churches to take episcopacy into their system. On the other hand, it is easy to see too how this could become a great bone of contention. When the report of these conversations was published in 1963, four of the Methodist representatives signed a minority report.[1] It reflected, no doubt, something of the antipathy to the ethos of the Church of England felt at the grass roots of Methodism. But it also pinpointed very important doctrinal objections to the kind of ways in which it was proposed to achieve acceptance of the historic episcopate in the scheme of union.

There was to have been a service of reconciliation framed in such a way that those who thought it necessary for Methodist ministers to be episcopally ordained were free so to interpret the laying on of hands which it included, while those who thought that there was no necessity for this as a condition without which reunion was unthinkable were free to interpret the rite in some less definite way.

Many of those who objected to the form of this service from an evangelical point of view believed that it was an offence against foundation principles of the gospel. They argued that it was not sufficiently different in essence from the situation envisaged by Paul's letter to the Galatians. There we find the apostle declaring that it was quite improper for Jewish Christians to impose circumcision on their non-Jewish fellow-believers. The argument he uses is that the real basis of unity between Jews and Gentiles is the cross of Christ. This, as is spelt out in Ephesians 2.14ff., is what has broken down the symbolic dividing wall in the Temple, because the only access to God, now that Christ has died, is through forgiveness offered by his atoning death: access equally available to all who look there for it. Just as it was wrong for Jewish Christians to impose circumcision on Gentile Christians as a condition of fellowship or full communion, so it is wrong to impose episcopal ordination as a prior condition of reunion between different denominations.

For this reason some evangelical Anglicans as well as some Methodists stood out against a scheme which obscured this truth. If any doubt whatsoever was cast on the integrity of free church experience of Christ and access to God, then nothing less than the heart of the gospel itself was threatened. But doubt of this kind is indeed cast wherever some other point than willingness to worship the crucified and risen Christ is made a focal condition of reconciliation, and wherever mutual participation in Holy Communion, which is the biblical and time-honoured symbol of reconciliation, is traded against some shibboleth of theological suzerainty.

Does this mean then that Methodist evangelicals are unwilling to accept bishops at all? Some of our number certainly take this position. They see monepiscopal orders as unrepresentative of the New Testament pattern of church leadership, or at least they would argue that other collegial models are found side by side with the kind of episcopal oversight exercised, say, by Titus in Crete. If pressed, they might even go so far as to say that acceding to pressure for Anglican-type episcopacy would be taking a dark step back into the Middle Ages, instead of moving even beyond the flexibility of free church order, such as it is, into the even more loosely knit and pragmatic pattern which arguably characterizes the New Testament and is likely to suit the fluid society of the twenty-first century. But while there are no doubt some who would take the hard line that on the day when Methodism accepts episcopacy they will abandon Methodism, there are others who do not regard the mere possession of or presence of bishops as an intolerable feature of a united church.

In the first place, the Church of England is in numerical strength bound to be the dominant partner in any foreseeable union. It is difficult therefore to see how a united church could be anything other than episcopal. The most that can be hoped for from a practical point of view is that episcopacy might be modified in such a way as to make its doctrinal definition more evangelical, and its outworking more efficient, notably by having smaller dioceses.

In the second place, the free churches mostly have figures whose function is similar to that of bishops in the Church of England. The real crux of the problem does not lie in the constitutional power possessed by the bishop (by whatever name he is known). For this is something that could, rather like the value of the pound, be expected to find its own level. It lies rather in the extent to which a particular understanding of episcopacy might be written into the formularies of any union.

The New Situation

However, the failure of the covenant has made these questions somewhat academic. What was embodied in its proposals probably failed more because it did not provide for a sufficiently explicit Anglo-Catholic understanding of the priesthood than because of misgivings in the Church of England about women in the ministry. But there was still the same ambiguity that bedevilled the service of reconciliation in the earlier scheme, and the Archbishop of Canterbury's influence in seeking modifications of the details in the proposals was directed towards stiffening the crucial prayer to make it more like an ordination. It was becoming a good question whether there was any significant improvement in the envisaged covenant by comparison with the previous scheme of union. Yet ironically, the failure of the proposals is likely to lead away from the possibility that anything as congenial to the Anglo-Catholic point of view will ever be considered in the ecumenical forum again.

The fact that there have been these two failures to suit a scheme to Anglo-Catholic scruples is itself significant. But it is fair to point out that the influence of this position in the Church of England is waning. The attempt was made in 1946 to defend the Anglo-Catholic view of the priesthood in a book edited by Bishop K. E. Kirk, *The Apostolic Ministry*.[2] This set out to prove that the historic episcopate was the sole legatee of the apostolic commission, in such a way that no non-episcopal community was entitled to call itself a church: 'The view that the ministry of word and sacrament in the Church of Christ can legitimately be exercised by any who have not received the commission to do so from the same unimpeachable source is unscriptural and un-apostolic'. J. I. Packer calls the book a lead balloon.[3] It failed and was seen to fail to be what it purported to be – a scriptural and historical demonstration of the view that bishops in this particular succession were essential not merely to the church's well-being but to a proper licence to be called the church at all.

One of the most significant contributions in the course of the deliberation of the Churches' Council for Covenanting was that of Father John Coventry, one of the Roman Catholic advisers. He argues that for a church which has the historic episcopate it should not be seen as essential to incorporate the ministry of any other church into it as a prior condition of reconciliation, since reconciliation by its nature actually effects this. It needs to be said frankly that this is not yet the official view of the Roman Catholic Church. It may require an abortive decade or perhaps a century of negotiations with the Church of England and to demonstrate that there is as little hope of a union between Rome and the Anglican Communions according to hardline 'Catholic' principles as there was between the Church of England and the Free Churches, so long as incorporation rather than reconciliation remained the dominant model for reunion. But the important thing to notice is that Father Coventry's position is the only view in the Roman Church which is compatible with the principles of the Church of South India union scheme. And the Church of South India union scheme is, significantly, one of the very few which have been realized.

The package of proposals which it consisted of, when the Church of South India came into being in 1947, was basically as follows:
(1) All ministers became accepted as ministers of the united church without any rite which could be interpreted as reordina-tion; (2) ordinations subsequent to reunion were to be carried out in a way which linked all new ministers to the historic episcopate; (3) a conscience clause was adopted to make it possible for a congregation which felt unsatisfied by a non-episcopally ordained minister to opt for one who had been ordained by a bishop.

In my view the principles of such a reunion are right, and it is only when the various parties involved on the English scene come to see it in this light that progress will be made in solving many of the ecumenical problems which confront us today. Of course the South India solution is open to the criticism that in a limited number of years the non-episcopally ordained ministers die off and then the church can become as rigorously episcopalian as the Church of England has tended to become as a result of the Oxford Movement. But against this, the original basis of union will be there to be remembered. And it is to be hoped that if ever such a union does take place, links of fellowship with churches at present in communion with one or another of the participants in that union will be maintained. With such safeguards it does not seem improper to allow this much for the scruples of those who would want to place a high value on the historic episcopate.

Those who may be sceptical about the doctrinal adequacy of such a way forward need to ponder the doctrinal adequacy of the present situation in England. Evangelicals who are often vociferous in their scepticism about schemes of reunion are as often unduly reticent about the current denominational scenario. Not that the variety of forms of worship should be an embarrassment; nor necessarily the number of churches on the ground. The real scandal is that inter-communion is in some places not even occasionally practised, and that there is no attempt made to co-ordinate the witness and outreach of neighbouring churches to make it clear to the world that they are all factors of the same organization rather than in independent competition with one another.

The approach which has been tried in the covenant has the advantage that it does not attempt to resolve overnight the morass of problems that arise with any scheme of organic reunion. But its failure may partly have been due to the extent to which it envisaged ultimate marriage as well as immediate engagement. It may be that the successor to the ill-fated covenanting proposals will be more open-ended. But the prophecy can be made with confidence that the pressure for closer relationships between the main denominations in England will not go away.

Scope for Unity at the Local Level

There are a large number of local ecumenical projects already and that number will grow. Their character requires that some attempt is made centrally to achieve what no local union can do by itself. Nevertheless, it would be a pity if this chapter were concerned only with an appraisal of the central negotiating scene, as if this were the only key to Christian unity. Certainly, one might legitimately complain that evangelicals have sometimes adopted an attitude of flying in the opposite direction, and giving the impression that central negotiations were beneath their contempt, or that structural re-unification of the denominational bodies was utterly misguided. It has been common to hear a damning contrast drawn between the kind of Christian unity which the Spirit brings to those who are true believers and what is derogatorily described as ecclesiastical carpentry.

There has always been a tendency among us, associated with this attitude, of sitting light to our denominational allegiance, and solving tensions which arise in the climate pervading the union proposals which we have had to consider in the past twenty years by abandoning our own church for a more doctrinally close-knit affiliation elsewhere. We have always tried to respect the consciences of those who felt led along this path, but at the same time we are sad at the way in which it has given rise to suspicion in, for example, the Methodist Church that evangelicals are forever growing wings in preparation for more or less imminent departure – a suspicion which can do nothing but foster the conviction that their interim presence need not be taken too seriously.

There is not room here to spell out the principles of legitimate secession. But they may be summarized in the following way. One ought to stay in a fellowship to which one belongs on the understanding that the relationship is part of God's providential leading, until such time as one is driven out, either forcibly, or by being required by further participation to act contrary to one's conscientious interpretation of God's will. One needs only to consider the maelstrom of heresies which characterized the earliest church to realize that the apostles who were responsible for the letters in the New Testament did not lightly abandon fellowships with which they had even major doctrinal disagreements. On the contrary such indications of denominational division as Paul detected in the church of Corinth he viewed with the utmost gravity and disapproval, while in other letters he set great store by the unity of Christians as fundamental evidence of the efficacy of the cross in destroying the barriers by which humanity is naturally divided.

While however, for these reasons, evangelicals have no need to be ashamed of taking part in the difficult quest for a solution to the denominational enigma in terms of mapping out guidelines centrally for progress towards the re-unification of the church, the present situation, in which such attempts have for the moment lapsed, argues for attention to be paid to the theatre of operations which exists at the local level.

Here we are confronted with four quite different situations. The inner city is the hardest area of all to evangelize, but for that reason among others, it is perhaps one of the easiest in which to co-operate with other denominations. Certain housing estates which are virtually unchurched present a similar aspect: whatever difficulties there may be, they are not those which arise from entrenched denominational loyalties.

But the Methodist Church consists largely of two other types of society: on the one hand, the kind of church which exists in the suburbs of a city or in a small town; and on the other, a large number of rural communities. It is important to see that for town churches no scheme of union generally poses a serious threat, provided that (as is in fact unthinkable) no attempt is made to impose uniformity of worship. In all towns of any size and in suburban situations it will be possible to argue that no offence is constituted to the principle of 'all in each place' by the continued existence of a number of centres for worship. One can imagine the notice board being altered to read 'United Church of England' and much else will continue as before. And even where this is not the case, and amalgamations take place, the homogeneity of suburban society makes it relatively easy for neighbouring churches to sink differences that never have been deeply theological.

The situation in the country is strikingly different. Here the Anglican Church has a much more dominant role in the community than it does in suburb or town. No doubt, as the decision to deploy the Church of England's manpower with greater respect to population density takes greater effect, an Anglican minister is becoming progressively more similar to his free church counterpart. But the fact remains that quite apart from the question of relative strength in terms of numbers, even if the count is confined to the electoral roll, the function of the parish church is very different from that of the chapel – except in parts of Norfolk and Yorkshire and elsewhere where the 'folk-religion' is Methodist rather than Anglican.

The effect of this is to make it very difficult to see how union can take place in rural areas except by the process of incorporating free churches into the Church of England. This prospect is a fearful one from the point of view of Methodists, and the question arises how its threatening elements can be avoided.

The danger is that as a result of such fears no progress will be made at all in areas of this kind. The need is therefore twofold. In the first place, free churchman and Anglican need to gain an insight into how the other thinks. The former will have to realize that enthusiasm for co-operation on the part of the latter is not necessarily to be interpreted as a take-over bid. And the latter will have to understand that it is precisely this fear which lurks in many non conformist minds, and gain a sympathy for the view that the demise of the chapel could mean an important loss in terms of variety of worship and closeness of fellowship.

The second need then is for a programme which will chip away at the intractable nut of disunity without posing the kind of threats which raise these fears. There are many things which can be done jointly which may be done already in separation: house-groups can become multi-denominational; it may be possible to have a united Sunday school or a joint prayer meeting. But it is even more important, and generally less threatening, to initiate new ventures. Certainly in country areas there is scope for pastoral care, which has often not been done at all, to be seen as something for which lay people are responsible. It may be possible to have a joint evangelistic mission or occasional guest services. Support for undenominational societies such as the Leprosy Mission, or a united approach to such annual events as Christian Aid Week also provides opportunities for increasing the strength of bonds between the churches in a village.

Conclusion

The movement towards church unity is one which inevitably

witnesses a great number of obstacles and set-backs. It is tempting for those who are temperamentally enthusiastic for progress to grow despondent whenever these arise. It is tempting, on the other hand, for others to feel relieved by such an event as the failure of the covenant, as though the storm has passed over without breaking. Neither of these attitudes is satisfactory. It is important to recognize that there is a real problem which needs to be grappled with, since there is no way in which denominational lines of division can be justified in the light of the spiritual unity which Christianity by its nature should create and foster. On the other hand, Christian unity must not be seen as a matter of all or nothing. Denominational divisions may not be justifiable, but they can often be the least of the threats to real unity. It is much more important that any one church should manifest signs of such wholeness and that any two or more churches should not be at daggers drawn with one another than that they should belong to the same outward organizational structure. This point puts in perspective the kind of disappointment that is appropriate when a scheme for reunion fails. There always remains much in this field that can and ought to be done.

Notes

1. *Conversations between the Church of England and the Methodist Church*, Church Information Office and the Epworth Press 1963, pp. 57–63.
2. K. E. Kirk, *The Apostolic Ministry*, Hodder and Stoughton 1946.
3. J. I. Packer, *Fellowship in the Gospel*, Marcham 1965, p. 13.

9

SOCIAL ACTION

David H. Howarth

According to Luke's Gospel, Jesus set the tone for his ministry with a quotation from Isaiah:

> The Spirit of the Lord is upon me, because he has chosen me to bring good news to the poor. He has sent me to proclaim liberty to the captives and recovery of sight to the blind; to set free the oppressed and announce that the time has come when the Lord will save his people (Luke 4.18, 19, quoting Isa. 61.1, 2, Good News Bible).

The question for Christians is not whether we ought to be involved in social action, but rather how we can share in Christ's continuing work of reconciliation and liberation. The very nature of contemporary society and of contemporary social issues demands alertness and awareness. We are constantly in situations where events are likely to overtake us if we are not alert and aware. Theories and warnings, facts and events confront each other in the most unexpected ways.

A recent example of the need for immediacy in responding to social problems came forcibly to the attention of the Methodist Conference of 1981. Included in its agenda were items concerning divisions between rich and poor within world society and national communities and questions as to our response under the gospel to these divisions. Did we recognize the existence of these divisions, what was our response to them, and what were we prepared to do?

As concern was being expressed by members of the Conference about the significance of the then recent incidents of riot proportions in socially deprived multi-racial communities of

Bristol and Brixton, news was received of similar incidents which were taking place at that very moment in Liverpool. At least one minister serving the area concerned, Toxteth, left Conference in order to exercise his ministry and to be of service on the spot in this time of great need and heightened tension.

The issue referred to above is also a good example of the need for both an immediate and a long-term response. Morris West indicates some basic considerations.[1] Such events as inner-city riots may be understood and defined in terms of a breakdown of law and order, or they may be seen as related to the concept of prophetic crisis, in which context they indicate the way things are going, express the consequences of social injustice, lack of understanding and failure of communication, and declare judgment upon a society that fails to respond adequately to the problems in its midst. The way forward can be a way of social change and liberation through a new understanding and its application. Our fundamental belief is that the gospel of God in Jesus Christ has the nature of that new understanding and application within it.

Some Basic Evangelical Responses

1. Historical

Evangelical social action has historically been somewhat paternalistic. Care, help and encouragement were given to many of the underprivileged and deprived of the last century. Often the work was done by well-endowed, well-intentioned individuals and groups, and mushroomed into large organizations. Nonconformist chapels in particular developed a pattern of activities designed to provide their members and young people with a real alternative to the life of 'the world'. For many people this proved to be a means of avoiding the problems posed by an increasingly secular society. Those who developed an acute social conscience sought to help actual and potential victims of that ruthless society. Mission churches sought to minister to many inner city dwellers. Those who were politically alert and proposed more radical solutions were deemed to be too materialistic in outlook.

It is within this framework of nineteenth century action that

we see developing the gospel/world tension so familiar to
evangelical Christians. But society had changed and was
changing dramatically. It was a mistake then, and it is a mistake
today, to assume that social action in the form of ameliorative
efforts is sufficient: what is required is a reappraisal and
modification of the social processes and structures. Evangelicals, of all people, committed as they are to the gospel of love
and salvation, must be prepared to advocate and facilitate its
influence and transforming power throughout society.

2. *Contemporary*

Evangelicals today remain loyal to the biblical and historical
roots of the evangelical tradition – particularly emphasizing the
biblical basis of faith and action, and personal experience of
Christ. A crucial dimension of contemporary evangelical belief
and practice is the attempt to develop a sound all-embracing,
socially aware theology.

The Universities and Colleges Christian Fellowship
(formerly the Inter-Varsity Fellowship of Evangelical Unions)
issued a journal, *Christian Graduate* now called *Christian
ARENA*, which featured a number of articles that illustrate this
point very clearly. The evangelical journal *Third Way*, first
published in 1977, seeks to develop understanding and action
based upon a biblical world view.

Journals are able to deal especially well with topical material,
but books give greater space for the development of ideas in
more permanent form. In works of differing scale and presenta-
tion, three British evangelical writers and one American offer a
good basic outline, together with helpful comment and suggestion.

Two former directors of the Shaftesbury Project (established
by a group of evangelicals for the exploration of Christian
involvement in society upon a biblical basis) have produced
valuable comprehensive and systematic introductions. Alan
Storkey[2] makes a valiant attempt to view social theory and
institutions in a Christian perspective, questioning the uncrit-
ical acceptance of secular approaches and interpretations as the
predominant if not exclusive ones. He argues for the recognition of a distinctive difference between the Christian faith
perspective and other perspectives, and spells this out in social

analysis. John Gladwin's book[3] is much more basic and less technical. He posits the relevance of biblical doctrine and ethics in relation to contemporary society and in the context of Christian and Marxist ideas of society.

Whilst both of these works may be described as practical, they do not seek to present any kind of social blue-print. Ronald Sider, founder-chairman of an American group, Evangelicals for Social Action, develops the argument in a different way and takes a world perspective. He argues that if we are to obey God as Lord of world and history, we cannot but see the need to change social attitudes and structures. Sider wrote *Rich Christians in an Age of Hunger*[4] and edited *Living More Simply*,[5] in which he explored biblical teaching and its implication for contemporary discipleship in terms of simpler life-style and also of social action directed against sin that is built into the structures of society.

Probably the most radical and revolutionary expression of theology in these days is found in the whole group of liberation theologies. Although there have been different variations upon this theme in subsequent years, the movement will always be associated with Latin America, where it originated.

It is no longer true, if indeed it ever was, that these expressions of theology can be seen as relating only to places beyond our shores. Twelve years of work in theological education in Argentina have given Andrew Kirk insights that he has now shared with a wider public. His *Liberation Theology – An Evangelical View from the Third World*[6] and *Theology Encounters Revolution*[7] guide us through the various expressions of liberation theology and issue a warning lest any kind of revolutionary theology should fail to give adequate biblical or christological bases to concerns of and for social justice.

In case it appears that only an extreme selection of writings is mentioned here, let it be said loud and clear that the more radically active and even aggressive stance is no forsaking of the gospel of peace and love and personal salvation, but rather a response to the urgency of the gospel and of the plight of God's loved ones, a response that we are obliged to adopt. It is a contemporary way of the cross.

As Jesus stood in the tradition of the Old Testament prophets in their stand for God's righteousness and for justice, so must his church. This realization is expressed in the Lausanne Covenant, which issued from the Lausanne Congress on World Evangelization of 1974. The covenant included this important paragraph, relating specifically to Christian social responsibility:

> We affirm that God is both the Creator and Judge of all men. We therefore should share his concern for justice and reconciliation throughout human society and for the liberation of men from every kind of oppression. Because mankind is made in the image of God, every person, regardless of race, religion, colour, culture, class, sex or age, has an intrinsic dignity because of which he should be respected and served, not exploited. Here too we express penitence both for our neglect and for sometimes having regarded evangelism and social concern as mutually exclusive. Although reconciliation with man is not reconciliation with God, nor is social action evangelism, nor is political liberation salvation, nevertheless we affirm that evangelism and socio-political involvement are both part of our Christian duty. For both are necessary expressions of our doctrines of God and man, our love for our neighbour, and our obedience to Jesus Christ. The message of salvation implies also a message of judgment upon every form of alienation, oppression and discrimination, and we should not be afraid to denounce evil and injustice wherever they exist. When people receive Christ they are born again into his kingdom and must seek not only to exhibit but also to spread its righteousness in the midst of an unrighteous world. The salvation we claim should be transforming us in the totality of our personal and social responsibilities. Faith without works is dead.
>
> Acts 17.26, 31; Gen. 18.25; Isa. 1.17; Ps. 45.7; Gen. 1.26, 27; James 3.9; Lev. 19.18; Luke 6.27, 35; James 2.14–26; John 3.3, 5; Matt. 5.20; 6.33; II Cor. 3.18; James 2.20.

This paragraph expressed a much more radical evangelical approach than that which had been seen in the 1960s, and provided a firm base for contemporary evangelical social thought and action, and indeed for contemporary radical evangelicalism. Moreover, whilst it would be foolish and naive to pretend or believe that there are only minor distinctions and differences between evangelical groupings, Roman Catholics, and the bodies under the umbrella of the World Council of Churches, the 1970s saw remarkable convergences of opinion and conviction.

Into Action – But on What Basis?

The attempt to move on from fundamental principles towards taking action may present all kinds of problems. It would in fact be nearer the truth to say that in making this attempt we shall inevitably meet problems. In order to face these we need to establish the basis on which we go forward and to apply this basis in our witness and action.

In basic terms the local church's role in social action is to seek to discover the areas and methods of activity and to be the vehicle for the equipping and supporting of its members in the tasks involved – as a body, or as individuals, or working with others. In specific terms this means prayerfully and thoughtfully considering the action required, determining how our resources can meet the demands of the situation, and understanding the social factors in that context. The fellowship should provide opportunities for free and mutually understanding dialogue between people of different backgrounds, opinions and convictions. Indeed it is in these areas that the church has a unique function as a unifying agency.

1. Bible and Doctrine

The evangelical assertion is that for this to be possible the biblical basis is essential. Although there may be subjective and unbalanced interpretations of scripture, there is within the Bible the definite guiding pattern of the progressive revelation. Existential and humanist frameworks are in danger of bypassing any such objective criterion. That is to say, from an evangelical standpoint the authority of the Bible as the revelation of the nature and will of God, and not simply human experiences and social trends, is the fundamental source of information and direction.

In the past evangelicals have been guilty of placing so much emphasis upon the doctrine of redemption that it has been seen as an isolated concept rather than as the central doctrine that they wished to emphasize. It has been the gathering point for ideas of personal salvation and individual ethics viewed almost completely in separation from the community. The principal failure has been that of being unable or unwilling to associate the doctrines of creation and redemption in a truly biblical way. Salvation and redemption are not experiences or doctrines to be seen out of context from life in general.

The God of the Bible is the Lord and giver of life, the one who gives true life (Gen. 2.7; John 6.25–58). He is the one who orders the creation and gives man responsibility over and within it (Gen. 1-2; Ps. 8). Whatever else may be derived from the first chapters of the Bible, the divine intention of harmony is indisputable. That intention persists as a theme of the Bible, and is reflected with a humanistic interpretation in nobler aspects of the history of mankind. The three dominant concepts of the Bible that may be related to it are those of *shālōm*, the kingdom, and life, taken respectively from the Old Testament, synoptic and Johannine strands of biblical literature.

Shālōm is a Hebrew word with no equivalent translation in a single form. Words such as wholeness or harmony perhaps begin to approach the idea. By definition it involves everything that is a positive expression of the harmony and balance and maturity that God intends for his people as central to their lives: well-being, growth, depth, fellowship, trust, peace. In the Old Testament it is said that the Messiah would embody this (Micah 5.5). Then Jesus comes and speaks of the kingdom (Mark 1.15) or of bringing life (John 10.10; 11.25).

Theologians see a clear association of ideas in these concepts, because they seem to be driving in the same direction and can legitimately be described as promise and fulfilment. They relate very much to anything we would say about social action. The outcome of all the discussions about whether this terminology is of this world or of the next is the conclusion that both are involved and that the life, death and resurrection of Jesus have bridged the gap that appeared between the two.

It is interesting to note that the late Leslie Weatherhead's book *In Quest of a Kingdom*,[8] which expounded the parables of the kingdom, bore on its dust cover the statement that it was 'an examination of Jesus' teaching on the kingdom of God, with special attention to the projected new world after the war'. Nevertheless, although this note on Weatherhead's book clearly shows the intention of demonstrating the practical application of Jesus' teaching, it was still seen from an individualistic standpoint. On the other hand, coming forward about thirty years, as we have seen, the various brands of liberation theology associated with Latin America are accused of superimposing a theology of salvation on to Marxist politics. Experience suggests that it is virtually impossible to reach a happy medium where individual salvation and Christian approaches to social change are happily and honestly related and worked out.

It is relatively simple to take, explore and expound biblical themes such as the sovereignty of God in creation, redemption and judgment, of man made in the divine image (with its practical implications of his being God's representative in the world and its theological implications of his sharing in the divine nature), and of the concepts of *shālōm*, the kingdom, and life; it is not so simple to work out a detailed social theology from them, let alone establish a valid pattern for Christian social action. Yet if we are to attempt to answer the question as to what is a Christian social order we must say that any answer is determined by the way in which the social order relates to these concepts. Similarly, the witness of individual Christians and groups of Christians, whether local, national or international, must be guided by these principles, for it is there that God's initial and continuing creative activity is declared. Since church communities and individual church members are set in a social context, the biblical teaching must be related to that context and to life experience. We cannot create relevance, but only expose it, and so there must be continual dialogue between on the one hand biblical teaching and theology and on the other those who belong to the church or seek to contribute to the dialogue from some other standpoint.

2. *Resources and Training*

Attempting to bring this down to practical matters in the life of a local church there are several suggestions that may be made. Today much emphasis is placed upon training, both initial and in-service, and the facilities for providing such opportunities are numerous. The church is in a very advantageous position in terms of premises, manpower and information where training is concerned. This is true not only of the national or regional organization, but equally of the local church.

The local church cannot do everything, of course. It needs the support of the larger body to provide material and information on a wider basis, and it needs also the resources of the local community. But one expression of the New Testament church as the body of Christ is the sharing of experience and knowledge on the part of its members in theory and in practice, and this is an important resource for social action.

Some Areas of Witness and Action

1. Work and Leisure

In an industrial society social action must be closely related to work. Questions of the Christian understanding of work and leisure, including the enforced leisure of unemployment, the nature of man, the exploration of newly discovered aspects of God's creation are all pertinent issues where the relevance of the biblical faith must be exposed and interpreted. Christian involvement in trade union activity and in industrial and commercial organization is a contribution to the guidance of people and movements in those areas.

2. Politics

Similarly, whilst there is no Christian political party in this country, there are committed Christians of most denominations in the membership of the major parties. It is quite clear that political and social organizations will develop that are anti-Christian or sub-Christian in tone and that there are areas of life in which Christians should have no part, where the fundamental doctrines already indicated are denied, but a Christian influence can shape the tone and policy of political parties and groups where there is opportunity to exert such influence.

3. Community Life

The churches are fortunate to be recognized as being entitled to representation on various councils and other bodies concerned with health, education and other social provisions. Sometimes such representation operates through local councils of churches, but there are also opportunities for individual churches to be represented. It is crucial that we take up every opportunity either by appointing the individual representative or by playing a full part in the appointing body such as a council of churches. In this way the local church can be kept alert to what is happening in the community and can establish the church's contribution.

4. *Home and Family*

It is important for a local church to accept its responsibility in maintaining the standards of Christian marriage and family life. This is possible through contacts with people in connection with marriage and baptism. In an age of a high divorce rate the standards of life-long marriage cannot be too greatly emphasized in marriage preparation and support to those married. When marriage breakdowns occur sympathy can be offered and grace shown, but this should not be at the expense of a total dispensing with Christian standards.

Questions relating to pornography and to human sexuality are persistently with us. Whilst the first may be dealt with fairly easily in terms of a rejection of any idea of endorsing the exploitation of sex, the other is a vexed question. The complexity of the subject requires understanding and knowledge in social, medical, psychiatric and theological aspects. There are no easy answers.

Serving in the Spirit of Jesus

In general terms the areas of social action to which we have referred deal with maintaining and developing a high quality of life and interpreting this in the light of biblical teaching and theological understanding. It is also to be seen in the context of an understanding of the nature and development of society and social institutions. This is accomplished through faithful and sincere attempts to be informed and to understand, through prayer, information and dialogue.

When action needs to be taken, this may be done by

individuals making their contribution with the support of their fellow-Christians, or it may be that the church can act as a body. The course of action will be determined largely by circumstances. Differing interpretations of situations and of teaching mean that in some circumstances a church may not be able to act as a unit.

I have already said that the traditional areas of social action on the part of individual Christians and of churches have been in terms of helping the afflicted. This is in tune with the ministry of Jesus, whose demonstrations of love and care towards social casualties and outcasts and whose healing miracles were signs of the presence of the kingdom and a fulfilment of the mission he announced in the synagogue at Capernaum. Attention to those in particular need is seen in the New Testament as an outworking of faith (cf. James 1.27). The social order may eventually be changed and injustices put right by political and social pressure on the part of individuals and/or groups, Christian and otherwise, but in the meantime the casualties need help. It may be that ultimately the solutions to the various social questions and ills are so complex that such action as takes place does not get very far and that we appear to find it much easier to analyse and discuss than to act. But there is action that can be taken. Indeed, if faith is genuine and responsibility is taken seriously, action must be taken. And to express faith and exercise responsibility in this way is to express the sentiments of *shālōm*, the kingdom, and life.

It is in many ways ironical and tragic that in a developed society with a great emphasis upon social provision so many slip through the net. There are many for whom the statutory services cannot provide; there are many more who cannot be provided for adequately. Some problems may be more predominant among members of one social group rather than another; others embrace people of various social groups. For example, in a society where people enjoy a longer life-span the loneliness and anxiety of ageing come eventually to innumerable men and women. Many churches express their beliefs about human dignity by offering service in this kind of area, either on a large or small scale, individually or corporately. In such circumstances action can certainly be ameliorative.

Sharing in God's Mission

When the life and mission of the Church generally or locally is under consideration the approach to the question too often seems to imply that everything is built around 'what *we* have decided to do'. We forget that mission is really God's expression of his love and purpose and that we share in that expression. God's mission is in bringing *shālōm* to his people. Social action is a part of the fulfilling of the mission. It is an aspect in which the whole church is involved. The task of the local church is to be firmly grounded in the principles of God's mission, to understand these principles and to apply them. The worship, prayer, fellowship and education of its members should point in that direction. The Church is an expression of *shalom* and as such is where people may come in order to discover and develop their role in mission. The task is to determine which course of action will be appropriate in which set of circumstances, and then to act accordingly. Whether they be acting individually or corporately, members of the church should accept, hear and support each other in fulfilling this calling, which is no less than the calling of God to his whole church.

Notes

1. Free Church Federal Council Annual Report for 1981 and Directory for 1982.
2. Alan Storkey, *A Christian Social Perspective*, IVP 1979.
3. John Gladwin, *God's People in God's World*, IVP 1979.
4. Ronald Sider, *Rich Christians in an Age of Hunger*, Hodder and Stoughton 1978.
5. Ronald Sider (ed.), *Living More Simply*, Hodder and Stoughton 1980.
6. Andrew Kirk, *Liberation Theology – An Evangelical View from the Third World*, Marshall, Morgan and Scott 1979.
7. Andrew Kirk, *Theology Encounters Revolution*, IVP 1980.
8. Leslie Weatherhead, *In Quest of a Kingdom*, Hodder and Stoughton 1943.

10

CHURCH GROWTH AND EVANGELISM

Geoffrey Jones

A Question of Balance

The relationship between evangelism and church growth can be compared to that between procreation and a happy family life. It is not possible to have a family at all without new life coming into the home, but having the new life does not guarantee a happy family that grows in every way.

Evangelism is concerned with increasing the size of God's family by making disciples, as our Lord Jesus Christ commanded us to do (Matt. 28.19). Without new disciples who put their trust in Christ and walk in his way the church would not continue. But church growth, which includes evangelism, embraces growth in many dimensions. It includes our growing up into a fuller knowledge of God, our growing together in unity and love as a body of believers, our growing out into the community as the influence Jesus called us to be there, and our growing more in numbers by bringing new disciples into the body of Christ.

A church that concentrates on only one of these elements to the neglect of the others will experience unbalanced life and witness. For example, a church that only evangelizes and is not concerned to build up those who confess faith in Christ will soon become weak in its witness in the community in which it is set. And churches that concentrate only on being an influence for good in their area and give little or no attention to evangelism and making disciples will soon decline.

The Bible clearly calls for both quality and quantity in our church life, and setting one against the other is not only time-wasting but sterile, and is increasingly seen to be so. The importance of both evangelism and other aspects of church growth has been more widely recognized, and there is a new expectation that the church of Christ in Britain will move forward and grow. Graphs indicating denominational decline are straightening out and some are rising. Evangelism is now on the agenda of almost all the church's life. At the same time there has been a quickened interest in the Church Growth Movement. Many denominations have had groups studying it, and independent agencies and missionary societies are making use of the Movement's findings.

Church Growth

The Church Growth Movement has made many Christians aware of the value of taking an in-depth and comprehensive look at their local church. By comparing what they find with what the Bible, church history and the contemporary growing world church teach us about the nature of the church, they are able to overhaul themselves in preparation for effective mission today. They are then able to pray, plan and act so that they may more nearly reach that standard.[1]

Scripture clearly assumes that God expects his church to grow (e.g. Matt. 16.18; 28.16–20; Acts 1.8; 2.41; 4.4). Most of our reluctance in Britain to face the challenge of seeing our churches grow arises, not so much from an ignorance or misunderstanding of biblical teaching, as from our sense of failure. We have sanctified decline and declared it to be the will of God. There has been a harsh doctrine of the righteous remnant underlying much thinking. We have almost come to believe that the smaller we are the more surely we are God's chosen people.

Such assumptions have been increasingly challenged as the Church Growth Movement has become more widely known. Donald McGavran's *Bridges of God*[2] launched the Movement in 1955, but it was not until fifteen years later, with the publication of the same author's *Understanding Church Growth*[3] and Alan Tippett's *Church Growth and the Word of God*,[4] that Church Growth became widely known in Britain.

The questions asked were predictable. Was this another American product seeking an English market? Was it cheap and nasty, and thus a temptation to avoid? Was it a formula for instant success based on business methodology, sociology and other worldly ideas? Or was it another bandwagon that people would jump on for a while and then jump off when it seemed no longer fashionable?

The Church Growth Movement has been caricatured in these ways, and many fail to realize how much this particular school of mission has to offer the declining British church. The Movement was born, not in America, as many believe, but in India, where research into how and why people became Christians was undertaken by a Methodist bishop, Dr Waskom Pickett, and Dr Donald McGavran. Evaluating the work of missions in their area, they asked such fundamental questions as: 'Why do some churches grow, while others in a similar context do not?' 'Why does the same church grow at one time and not at another?' 'Why do some parts of the church grow while other parts do not?' Those are questions worth asking in any country at any time.

1. Principles and Methods

How churches grow, the researchers found, was no simple matter. They examined each church's background, analysing the area in which it was set, the type of people living there, their culture, their needs, their problems. They looked carefully at the church itself, its leadership, teaching, methods, membership, structure and management.

Both researchers compared what they found with what the Bible taught about the ongoing mission of the church. Where biblical principles were being followed at district and local levels the result was the kind of growth seen in the early church. When biblical principles were neglected, decline was seen.

In addition, the more complex principles of human behaviour had to be faced. Methods that did not take into account the kind of people the church was dealing with, from their great variety of backgrounds, failed to be effective. Programmes and methods that ignored cultural differences in the rich mosaic of Indian society lost the church potential disciples. The insensitive use of methods that assumed all people were alike created their own problems. Missionaries who failed to recognize their Western cultural biases when dealing with Asian culture were far too common.

So the principles that help churches grow must be biblical and the methods matched to the situation. The church must be culturally sensitive and adaptable in its approach to mission.

It must also be prayerful. The dynamic of the Church Growth Movement is that the Holy Spirit, who inspired the scriptures, and therefore revealed the principles, equips us to make disciples of all nations. He will provide the spiritual resources and power necessary, if we obey him.

2. *Factors in Growth and Decline*

Many church leaders involved in the Church Growth Movement have experienced a recovery of faith and hope. But this has come only after they have taken an honest and searching look at their personal lives and at the life of their church. They have had to face facts and emerge from the fog that so often blurs our vision and hides the truth.

The church can be seen as a living organism whose state of health needs to be checked, for positive signs that point to healthy growth, and for pathological symptoms of decline.

Among the best known analyses of the signs of health is that by C. Peter Wagner in his *Your Church Can Grow: Seven Vital Signs of a Healthy Church*.[5]

Wagner believes that:

(1) The minister is the primary catalytic factor for growth if he is a possibility thinker and a dynamic leader.

(2) The growing church will have a well-mobilized laity which has discovered, developed and is using all the spiritual gifts of the church for growth.

(3) It needs to be big enough to provide a range of services that meets the needs and expectations of its members.

(4) It needs to provide its members with corporate experiences at three different levels: celebration, where larger numbers add a new dimension to worship, congregation, a church-based peer group where all know one another and experience at least social fellowship, and cell, a group of about eight to twelve meeting for spiritual fellowship.

(5) The membership of a healthy growing church is composed basically of the same kind of people (the 'homogeneous unit principle', which many would question).

(6) A growing church uses evangelistic methods which are

known to work.

(7) A growing church gives evangelism and care of new converts a higher priority than social action.

Paul Beasley-Murray and Alan Wilkinson have carried out a careful investigation of the relevance of these 'seven vital signs' to the British scene in *Turning the Tide: An Assessment of Baptist Church Growth in England*.[6]

Another British writer, Roy Pointer, in *How Do Churches Grow?* has listed ten signs of growth, which he summarizes as follows:

> Churches grow when they pray constantly; respect the authority of the Bible; appoint effective leaders; mobilise their membership; worship God in eventful services; engage in continuous evangelism and compassionate service; develop genuine community life; are open to Spirit-directed change and release the resources of the church for the mission of God.[7]

Such analyses of growth factors provide check lists that can be discussed with sensitivity and honesty by the leaders of any church seeking to grow. But besides these signs of health to be looked for, there are diseases of decline that need diagnosing if the symptoms show themselves. What percentage of church members are seemingly concerned mainly with keeping the church open? Are new ideas consistently blocked by the formula 'We've tried it before and it didn't work'? Is the difference between what the church claims to be and what it appears to be to those around it creating a credibility gap? Is there much huddling together of Christians, but little taste for going out to share the faith with others? Is the church lacking in youthful leadership and activity?

Some Church Growth writers have given some of these 'diseases of decline' intriguing titles such as 'maintenance complex', 'failure syndrome', 'fellowshipitis', 'remnantitis' and 'people blindness'. Behind the jargon are serious questions that any church would do well to ask itself. Among the writers who have been most penetrating in their analysis of these diseases is Eddie Gibbs in his *Body Building Exercises for the Local Church*.[8] These 'exercises' have taught many British churches how to arrest decline and begin to grow.

3. Goals of Ministry

A church that has faced realistically what it is now will need also to decide what sort of church it wants to be. A careful look should be taken at what gifts God has placed in the people in the church so that these can be compared with what use has been made of them in the past.

Another vital piece of research must be undertaken, into the composition of the community in which the church is set. Maps of the area and census returns can be studied and compared with church figures to see what match or mismatch there is.

It should be possible then to make faith projections. These should be carefully prepared, with all section leaders being brought in to give their individual guidance as to what they feel is a realistic, relevant and faith-requiring goal for each of their ministries. They need to make these goals their own, and some kind of accountability needs to be written into the faith projections. This will involve being specific about numbers and about a time scale at each stage.

When goals have been set and accepted and strategies worked out, then the membership of the church must be mobilized to pray, believe and act with a view to achieving, by God's power, the goals they believe he has led them to accept.

Evangelism

Evangelism was on the church's agenda long before Church Growth as a movement was heard of. Church Growth, far from distracting attention from evangelism, has set it in context and quickened interest in its effectiveness. It is seen as vitally important that the church that is seeking to grow should agree about its goal of evangelism and find and use methods that actually make disciples. To find such methods will involve much careful planning and believing prayer.

1. The Role of All God's People

For a church to grow by making new Christians, a model needs to be adopted where the minister encourages, helps and if possible leads in evangelism, and all the laity are involved.

Evangelism is not an optional extra for those with an evangelical turn of mind; it is a mandate for every Christian. All

God's people are called to be involved in the evangelistic task of the church. While some have special gifts as evangelists, all who know Christ have the responsibility to share this faith and testimony. The importance of every Christian's witnessing in all the areas of life and within the network of existing relationships cannot be overstressed. It has been estimated that eighty-five per cent of those who come to Christ and then join the church have been won within friendship and kinship circles.

Christians are not, however, likely to feel the need to engage in personal evangelism unless they are highly motivated by their own experience of Christ. Nothing can be more vital in the area of promoting direct witness than helping Christians to become grounded in the word of God, in prayer and in walking the Christian way close to Christ. Those who feel called to invest their lives in other people to enable them to grow in this way are precious in the life of the growing church. This is sacrificial, demanding and effective work. Those so trained usually become spiritual leaders of a high calibre, with a vision of, in their turn, investing *their* lives in those who are younger in the faith than they are.

2. *Training in Faith-sharing*

In addition to training in discipleship, would-be witnesses need specific training in faith-sharing. We will mention a few of the many methods God seems to be using in these days to mobilize and equip Christians for their role.

James Kennedy's 'Evangelism Explosion' programme originated in America, but is now being used in Britain under the title 'Teach and Reach'.[9] The Church Pastoral-Aid Society Mission at Home's 'Operation Breakthrough' provides a kit for self-help training in evangelism.[10] Good suggestions are given in the Grove Booklet *Good News Down the Street*.[11] Bryan Gilbert's 'One Step Forward' is a programme that includes the whole church in its thinking and puts forward an effective strategy for evangelism and church growth.[12]

It is not only in personal evangelism that lay men and women can be called on to share their faith. Those who have a testimony to give and a gospel to make known can be drawn together into witness teams to spearhead the proclamation of Christ in local church services and, as they are invited, to move

around a circuit or district. On a wider scale still, the Lay
Witness Movement has much to commend it, with its method
of inviting a team of men and women drawn from a wide area to
visit churches for a week-end of caring and sharing.[13]

3. Old but Not Obsolete

Some time-honoured methods of evangelism have recently
been revived in new forms. One of these is open-air preaching,
as old as the New Testament, but long neglected for lack of
response. In some areas this has become powerful again, with
the use of sketch boards, guitars, street theatre, a conversa-
tional word, and a team of people ready among the listeners to
turn and share their faith with them.

The use of literature in evangelism has moved far since the
days of unattractively printed tracts. Christian presses are
producing modern version Bible portions in artistically designed
colour leaflets, as well as short readable books, equally well
produced, some beamed on the literary and some on the non-
literary reader. Testimony books telling of people living today
whose lives Christ has transformed have been the means of
opening many eyes to see what Christ can do. Gospel newspapers
such as *Challenge*,[14] printed in the same format as tabloids, also
tell of what God is doing in lives today. Bookstalls are seen at the
back of churches and at public meetings of all kinds. Book parties
in homes, run on the lines of those arranged to sell kitchenware or
cosmetics, are the means of getting Christian literature,
including Bibles and children's books, into fresh homes.
Literature is an invaluable tool for evangelism if it is used well,
and has a crucial part to play in the witness of the local church.

Visitation evangelism is made more difficult by people's
absorption with television, but need not therefore be aban-
doned. Door-to-door calls may best be paid in harness with
fellow-Christians from other churches. The local church may
decide to concentrate on contacts made through baptisms,
weddings, funerals, Sunday schools, mid-week activities, and
special services. It is good to look first for receptive people and
focus on them, whilst not neglecting others.[15]

4. The Preacher's Role

Evangelism in the local church depends a good deal on the

kind of worship and preaching in the Sunday services. Research in this country has proved that most of the growing churches have inspiring worship that is relevant, up to date, happy and God-glorifying. The minister in the growing church is not necessarily a great preacher, but one who understands what he is doing and who preaches the word of God faithfully. It is vital that, as people are being newly introduced to the church by their friends, the pulpit should have no uncertain sound, but that they hear a clear and constant emphasis on the gospel of our Lord Jesus Christ. They need also a teaching element that presents the reality of Christian living to which they are being asked to commit themselves.

In many places family services and guest services are growing in popularity and are bringing new faces into the church. An opportunity is lost if family services are conducted only as if they were children's services. At guest services suitable music and testimony can be arranged and preachers invited who can take full advantage of the mission situation and seek to lead people to a clear response to God's offer of new life in Christ.

From time to time methods such as those that have already been mentioned may culminate in a special time of concentration, with specialist preachers and communicators. Such a period of mission will be different in many ways from those of the past, but it still has a part to play in the evangelistic strategy of the church.

Occasionally there is the opportunity for a church to join in a major programme of evangelism that attracts media interest, such as those of Billy Graham and Luis Palau. It has been found again and again that the churches that see most church growth at such times are those that have thrown their weight behind them as though the evangelist were coming to their churches and have prepared for the nurture of those responding.

5. *Preparing for After-care*

There is a growing recognition that for evangelism to be effective, the follow-up must be given as much attention as the build-up, and must be carefully provided for beforehand. Studies of group dynamics have shown that if a group increases quickly, unless there are structures already prepared to receive additional numbers, it will eventually return to its original size.

Two things may have happened: new people may have come, and not been cared for or properly integrated, or the original people may have left, feeling threatened by the increased size, or by the newcomers. Hence the need for carefully-planned pastoral structures to accommodate growth.

Churches seriously preparing to receive new Christians soon become aware of the need to improve the devotional life of their congregations, both at the individual and group levels. Those who have made profession of faith are in urgent need of help in understanding and consolidating their commitment, and of training in personal discipleship, witness and service. This follow-up may, for the first six weeks or so, best be provided for each by an individual Christian to whom the church has given responsibility for doing this.

After an initial period of personal follow-up, or overlapping it, there will need to be a welcome or nurture group into which the new Christian can move. If many new Christians are being received a twelve-week church membership course may be kept running throughout the year. Newcomers are drafted in at whatever point the group has reached, and continue round the whole twelve sessions of the carousel, as it has sometimes been called.[16]

There may be a need for small groups of different kinds that will provide for different types of people and for varying needs. It is good for new Christians to mix with and learn from more established believers, but it should be recognized that most fellowships are neither geared to evangelism nor suitable to put new Christians in immediately after they have come to faith.

6. *The Cost of It All*

It must be clearly stated that there is no blueprint for growth and that methods that work in one place do not necessarily succeed in another. But a vision for growth can provide a framework within which one person may lead, and others take up the vision and follow. It can point to certain avenues of service and outreach that will stimulate the life and growth of the local church.

What happens next will largely depend upon the personal discipleship of those who take up these ideas and use them. Jesus made it clear that if we remain united to him, he will remain united to us, and we shall bear much fruit. He will go on to prune us so that we may bear more fruit (John 15.1–4, Good News Bible).

Christians cannot expect this to be an easy process. It involves being crucified with Christ, denying oneself to follow him, taking up one's cross, seeking first the kingdom of God. But people cannot be won to Christian discipleship and integrated as believing, learning, loving and witnessing members of Christ's body the Church by anything less than total dedication on the part of many people.

Both church growth and evangelism depend in the end upon the way Christians in the local church love Jesus Christ and serve him with all their hearts.

Notes

1. For a comprehensive account of present Church Growth thinking see Eddie Gibbs, *I Believe in Church Growth*, Hodder and Stoughton 1981.

2. Donald McGavran, *Bridges of God*, World Dominion 1955.

3. Donald McGavran, *Understanding Church Growth*, Grand Rapids, Michigan, Eerdmans 1970.

4. Alan Tippett, *Church Growth and the Word of God*, Grand Rapids, Michigan, Eeerdmans 1970.

5. C. Peter Wagner, *Your Church Can Grow: Seven Vital Signs of a Healthy Church*, Glendale, California, Regal Books 1976.

6. Paul Beasley-Murray and Alan Wilkinson, *Turning the Tide: An Assessment of Baptist Church Growth in England*, Bible Society 1981.

7. Roy Pointer, *How do Churches Grow?*, Marshall, Morgan and Scott 1979.

8. Eddie Gibbs, *Body Building Exercises for the Local Church*, Falcon 1979.

9. Evangelism Explosion, 228 Shirley Road, Southampton, SO1 3HR.

10. CPAS Mission at Home, Falcon Court, 32 Fleet Street, London, EC4Y 1DB.

11. Michael Wooderson, *Good News Down the Street*, Grove Pastoral Series No. 9, Grove Books 1983.

12. One Step Forward Ministries, High House, Walcote, Lutterworth, Leicestershire. LE17 4JW.

13. Lay Witness Movement, 20 Victoria Road, Burbage, Hinckley, Leicestershire. LE10 2JG.

14. Challenge Literature Fellowship, Revenue Buildings, Chapel Road, Worthing, West Sussex, BN11 1BQ.

15. For a practical survey of some effective methods of evangelism see *Methods of Mission*, ed. Brian R. Hoare Methodist Publishing House, for the Home Mission Division of the Methodist Church 1979.

16. Roy Pointer, op. cit., pp. 139, 140, gives a useful model for elementary instruction of new Christians.